LIFE IN REGENCY AND EARLY VICTORIAN TIMES

PLATE I.

A BANQUET AT THE ROYAL PAVILION, BRIGHTON.
[from the coloured lithograph by Joseph Nash

LIFE IN REGENCY AND EARLY VICTORIAN TIMES

AN ACCOUNT OF THE DAYS
OF BRUMMELL AND D'ORSAY
1800 to 1850

By
E. BERESFORD CHANCELLOR
M.A., F.S.A.

Author of "The XVIIIth. Century in London," etc.

CLASSIC EDITIONS

This edition digitally re-mastered and
published by JM Classic Editions © 2007
Original text © E Beresford Chancellor 1926

ISBN 978-1-905217-78-6

All rights reserved. No part of this book subject
to copyright may be reproduced in any form or
by any means without prior permission in writing
from the publisher.

PREFACE.

THE present volume may in a sense be said to be supplementary to my book entitled "The 18th Century in London," which appeared during the winter of 1920 and which, owing to the interest now taken in the past history of the capital, had a remarkable success. In that work I endeavoured to outline the architectural development and social life of London from 1700 to 1800. In the present work, the scheme is somewhat similar, but under the changed conditions which obtained from 1800 to 1850. During the first half of that period the influence of Brummell and the group of Dandies surrounding him, was at first directly and afterwards indirectly, paramount on the habits and dress of the more decorative class of citizens; in the second half that influence had passed into the hands of D'Orsay and *his* set; and so these two outstanding men may be taken as protagonists representative of the two portions of the selected period.

It need hardly be said that there are innumerable characteristics in the annals of this era which do not come specially under the sway of the Dandies—whether represented by Brummell or D'Orsay—such as the life of the people generally; their amusements and "follies," often as insistent as those of the great; the architectural developments of these years; the life of outstanding provincial centres; and a variety of other subjects not immediately connected with fashionable life, although they receive that attention which as component parts of a great whole, they deserve.

The period is one of absorbing interest, and one, besides, that wedged as it were between the 18th century and the later 19th century, both so full of incident, is apt to be overlooked. It was a time of transition, and as such affords to the observer of manners and customs a very fascinating study. The old order survived with modifications till the accession of Queen Victoria; while what we term the early Victorian era covered just that period from 1837 to 1850 when a more modern conception of life began to obtain, and when new ideas were being formed and, in many cases, consolidated.

During the first quarter of the century the Georgian convention held sway. The habits and customs of the latter years of George

PREFACE.

III's reign, still persisted, although in a modified and gradually changing way. The dress of the earlier portion of the time presented much similarity with the fashions which had preceded it ; in manners and customs alterations were here and there obvious, but were only slowly making themselves felt, and such survivals of a former barbarism as the baiting of animals, emanating from a species of boisterous delight in blood-letting, were still rampant. As usual such things depended largely on the patronage of the great for their success and continuance, and with the advent of Brummell, much as that extraordinary man has been sneered and laughed at, there is no doubt that an emollient to rough and ready manners made itself felt, and largely, if often indirectly, through his influence. Gaming went on unabated, but it had taken on a cloak of outward restraint and breeding. In place of Ranelagh with its licence came Almacks with its exclusiveness. Human nature was, as always, the same, but the dress it wore was, actually and metaphorically, a more subdued one.

In place of the wits of the earlier Georgian day—the Walpoles and Selwyns, the Storers and the Herveys, we have the Luttrells and Alvanleys, the Theodore Hooks and the Sydney Smiths. The "Salon" in the hands of such leaders of fashion as Lady Holland and Lady Blessington really began to be a power in the social life of London.

Literature had passed from the domination of Johnson and his great circle to the gentler, more urbane, dictates of Lamb and Scott and that splendid constellation which was, in this respect, with Dickens and the rest, destined to make the earlier half of the Victorian Era memorable.

With the accession of the young Queen, the changes which had gradually been over-spreading the country, suddenly began to move with startling rapidity. Decency in Court life gave the cue to decency in other social circles, down to the lowest, and an entirely new era was inaugurated on that famous 20th of June, 1837 which saw the end of the old order of ruler as surely as it did the old order of social life.

In such a work as the present, much in this dual period can only be touched upon allusively, for hardly has any half century been so full of marked development as this which began with George III on the throne and closed with the first thirteen years of his granddaughter's rule. I have, however, in spite of many obvious

PREFACE.

difficulties, which it would be mere affectation to ignore, attempted to give such a general picture of the time as will, I hope, enable the reader to judge how full and pregnant with events and with outstanding personalities it was.

As decorative aids to this end, a mass of illustrations has been traced and selected, showing the salient features of the times as exemplified in its social, literary, artistic and what may be termed, its general features. The London and some of the outstanding provincial centres of the period are thus recorded, in a way that enables us at a glance to gain a knowledge of their appearance and of that of those who perambulated their streets or were notable in their social and official life. The stage coach gives place to the tentative railway; top boots and brocaded waistcoats disappear before the trouser and the top-hat; Mr. Brummell passes away in favour of Count D'Orsay; the rule of Carlton House is merged in that of Buckingham Palace; while the effulgent first gentleman of Europe is happily replaced by that young Queen, to whom, as Thackeray once said, in a notable passage, " I am sure the future painter of our manners will pay a willing allegiance, and be loyal to the memory of that unsullied virtue."

E. BERESFORD CHANCELLOR.

London,
    September, 1926.

NOTE OF ACKNOWLEDGMENT.

Many of the illustrations in this book have been reproduced by the courtesy of dealers from whose collections they have been taken, and especial thanks are due in this respect to Messrs. Ellis & Smith, of Grafton Street, W., Messrs. Rimells of Duke Street, and Shaftesbury Avenue, W., and Messrs. Walford Brothers of New Oxford Street, W.C., who have on several occasions given the publishers access to much important material. Thanks are also due to Messrs. Walker Bros., of Bond Street, W., Mr. Basil Dighton of Savile Row, W., and Mr. E. A. Lindow, of Brompton Road, S.W., for allowing the reproduction of various prints and drawings from their respective collections.

The Publishers have also to thank Mr. Edward Knoblock for allowing them to photograph and reproduce the interiors at No. 11, Montague Place, W.; Mr. J. L. Douthwaite, of the Guildhall Library, for the loan of prints from his private collection, and for his valuable advice in research work on the illustrations; and Mr. Angus Brodie for the loan of several prints from his collection. The remainder of the subjects have in most cases been selected from originals in the British Museum, Victoria and Albert Museum, London Museum, Guildhall Museum and Library, and from the Publishers' own collection.

By George Cruikshank.

CONTENTS.

Chapter		Page
I	General Aspects of London:	
	(i) Manners and Modes	1
	(ii) "Stucco and Paint"	12
II	The Reign of the Dandies	24
III.	Social Centres	39
IV.	Gaming and Gamesters	59
V.	Art and Literature:	
	(i) Art	70
	(ii) Literature	78
	(iii) Music	82
	(iv) The Theatre	84
VI.	Fun and Frolic	87
VII.	Health Resorts	110
	Index	124

Chapter I.
GENERAL ASPECTS OF LONDON.
I.—MANNERS AND MODES.

IT is easier to reconstitute the outward appearance of the London of the first half of the 19th century, although its constant architectural changes make this no light task, than to present a picture of the life of the streets during such a time of evolution. So many marked differences occurred between the manners and customs of the citizens of the early years of the new century and the later, that one finds it well-nigh impossible to realise that we are dealing with the same people who in 1800, wore buckskin breeches, large brimmed round hats, and long-tailed, deep-collared coats; and who in 1840, sported trousers and overcoats and hats, not markedly dissimilar from those now in fashion. If you take a picture by Rowlandson or a caricature by Gillray and compare it with, say, the figures in one of Phiz's illustrations to contemporary novels or one of Boys' beautiful views of London, you will see at a glance what a change had come over the dress and appearance of the male sex during the first half of the 19th century. The mere man hesitates to enlarge on ladies apparel, not only because it is a vast and complicated subject, but also because the vagaries of fashion are so responsible for a throw-back to earlier modes, that dates do not always accurately show development in this direction; but a glance at the accompanying fashion plate (Plate 3) will afford a comparative idea of the essential changes that took place during the period.

The life of the streets exhibits changes as marked and various. Practically during the whole of the time the old turnpikes, which gave such a distinctive note to various parts of London—Hyde Park Corner; the north end of Park Lane; and elsewhere—existed, and when Lord Nelson spoke of the Piccadilly Gates, a remark that has given rise to much conjecture, I think he was but referring to the turnpike that remained close to Apsley House till 1825. As we are at this corner of London, I note the fact that Decimus Burton's screen (Plate 2), set up here in 1828, may be taken as marking the most drastic change that has occurred at this spot—a spot then notable to many a Londoner and visitor to

LIFE IN REGENCY AND EARLY VICTORIAN TIMES

London, because of the almost daily sight afforded by the Iron Duke as he mounted his horse at the door of ' No. 1 London,' for his ride in the Park.

Another "sight" was that afforded by the old "Charlies," the picturesque but hardly adequate guardians of the peace, who perambulated the town or took their ease in their boxes (when they were not being overturned by roystering young bloods) (Plate 11), and who were superseded, in 1829, by the regular police force, known as Peelers or Bobbies, from the fact that Sir Robert Peel was responsible for their creation. The detective force was then represented by the Bow Street Runners, of whom Townshend (who appears in many caricatures, as well as in Dighton's excellent portrait) was the most famous.

Fires then as now collected their agitated crowds, but the fire engines in force were very different from those to which we are accustomed. In the museums you may see these archaic precursors of the modern idea: lumbering little machines, worked by hand, and even in days when houses did not reach the altitude they now attain, seemingly almost useless in coping with anything but the mildest of conflagrations.

In those days all sorts of things contributed to what may be termed passing amusement. The era saw, for instance, three coronations, that of George IV being perhaps the most splendid that had ever taken place. Anything of this sort was responsible for innumerable pictures and prints, and we can realise from the reproductions here given, how gorgeous and extensive must have been that portion of the show exhibited to Londoners (Plates 61 and 62); while inside the Abbey, the relatively favoured few faced the glory of the First Gentleman in Europe in his apotheosis— an apotheosis to which the fly in the ointment was afforded by the ill-used Queen's attempt to gain admittance. That Queen was the centre of many an ovation, for if the people did not exactly love her, they so disliked her husband that they never allowed an opportunity to pass without exhibiting a sort of fictitious regard for the injured lady: whether she was hammering at the door of the Abbey; going to and from her scandalous trial; visiting Alderman Wood in St. James's Square; or coming to and fro between Blackheath or Brandenburgh House at Hammersmith.

The more regular amusements of the people differed naturally according to their status in society; except in the matter of cock-

The Grand Western Entrance to Hyde Park.
Decimus Burton's New Archway (1831)

By H. Brooks

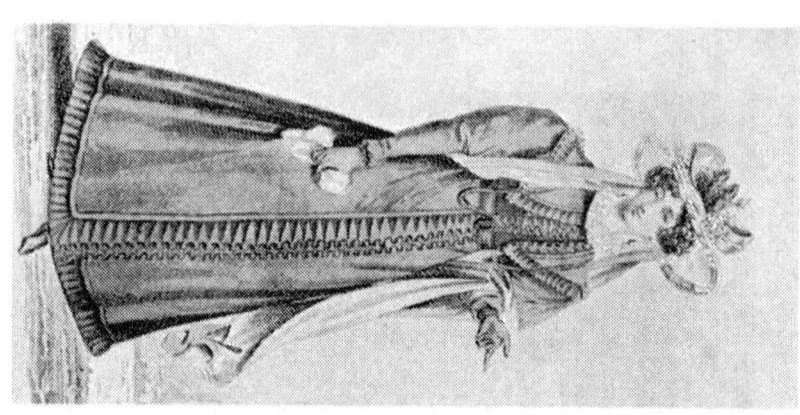

Day Dress (1827)

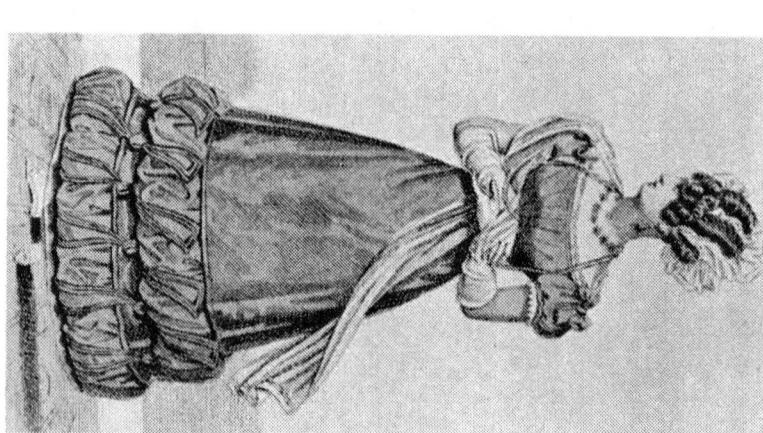

Evening Dress (1827)

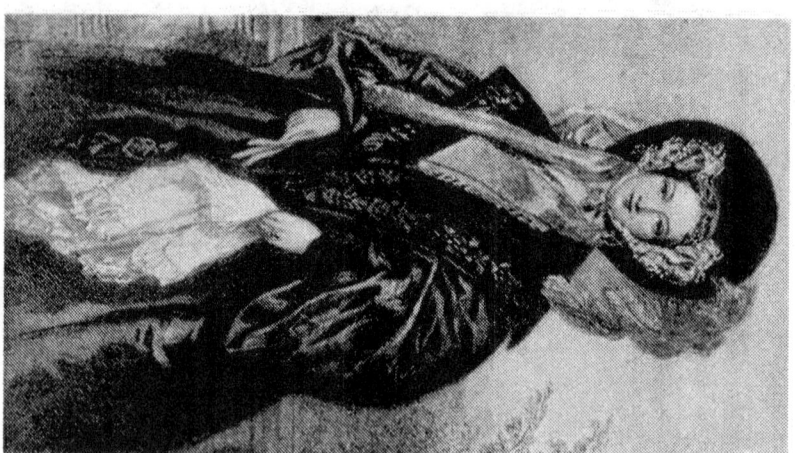

The Fashion for 1845
A Portrait of Lady Blessington by Chalon

REGENCY AND EARLY VICTORIAN FASHIONS

A VIEW OF CHARING CROSS IN 1807

By G. B. Moore

The Pantheon Bazaar, Oxford Street
By C. J. Richardson

A London Tea-Merchant's Shop
By G. Scharf

fighting and the prize-ring, where all classes assembled, and the noble hob-nobbed with the cit or even with the denizen of Seven Dials and Whitechapel with the utmost nonchalance. During the earlier years of the period, many of those semi-barbaric forms of enjoyment which had obtained during the 18th century survived; but during the efflux of time a more restrained air is observable in the amusements of the people who seem to have left it to their betters to astonish the city with mad and daring vagaries. The theatre became much more a part of civic life than it had hitherto been, and although, compared with what we have to-day, playhouses were limited in number, at the same time they were far more numerous than they had been during the preceding century, and they catered for a far wider audience. Drury Lane and Covent Garden were the chief temples of histrionic art, but there was also the Olympic, in Wych Street, opened in 1816 by Philip Astley; the Little Theatre in the Haymarket, which closed its doors during the autumn of 1820; the Theatre Royal, next door, which opened in the summer of 1821; and the Opera House opposite. There was also the Royalty Theatre, in far-flung Wellclose Square which, in 1819 or thereabouts, after being shut up for some years, was re-opened as the East London Theatre, but was burnt down (the usual destiny of playhouses, it would seem) in 1826; and the Brunswick Theatre, which met a similar fate a couple of years later, after having just been rebuilt. There was, too, Sadler's Wells (Plate 48), where Charles and Mary Lamb used to go (the latter describes a performance here, in a letter dated 1803); and the Pantheon, in Oxford Street, rebuilt by Cundy in 1812, and serving alternately as a theatre, an opera house and a general assembly room (Plate 48) —far different from its splendid career during the earlier years of George III's reign. In addition to these may be mentioned the Strand Theatre or Non-Pareil, as it was called, opened in 1802, and enlarged twelve years later; the Lyceum, to which Crabb-Robinson once went with Lamb, in 1811; the Regency Theatre, in Tottenham Street, on the site of the rooms of the "Ancient Music" patronised by George III, where Colonel Greville, in 1802, instituted his Pic Nic Society, and which was subsequently to become the "Prince of Wales's"; while on the south side of the river, were the Coburg Theatre first opened in 1818; and the Surrey Theatre which, originally inaugurated in 1782, had been burnt down, re-opened in 1799, again burnt to the ground in 1805, but re-built and re-opened on Easter Monday, 1806. Nor should one forget Astley's Amphitheatre which, like most places of amusement, was destined to be consumed by fire, but to arise Phœnix-like from its own ashes.

During the summer months the many tea gardens which had flourished during the preceding century, and certain of which continued to enjoy public favour well on into the new one, were the resorts of the citizen. Marylebone and Cuper's Gardens had ceased to exist before the beginning of the 19th century, and Ranelagh only survived till 1803, but Vauxhall continued more or less prosperously till 1859, and with its thousands of lamps, its miraculously thinly-cut ham, its rack-punch (so disastrous to Jos. Sedley on a famous occasion), and its protagonist, C. H. Simpson, continued to enjoy public favour. Before it closed, Rosherville Gardens had become well established (they were opened in 1837); and Cremorne had commenced (1843) its thirty odd years of successful enterprise. Such places as Bagnigge Wells which closed in 1841, and the White Conduit House which ceased to exist eight years later, as well as Highbury Barn which lingered on till the seventies, although survivals from 18th century enterprise, had so altered in the character of the attractions they offered to the public, that their originators would hardly have recognised them. Malcolm who wrote in 1803[1], mentions Islington Spa, or the New Tunbridge Wells as it was called, with enthusiasm, and among other resorts, given in the Picture of London for 1818, by Leigh, who speaks of them as " frequented by the middling classes, on Sunday especially," may be recorded Hornsey Wood House and Tea Gardens; Canonbury House; Bayswater Tea Gardens; Copenhagen House, Pentonville; The Shepherd and Shepherdess Tea Gardens, City Road; Hoxton Tea Gardens; the Yorkshire Stingo, in Lisson Grove; the New Ranelagh, Millbank; the Kilburn Tea Gardens, Edgware Road; and a variety of other similar places of resort for the citizen and his family.[2]

It must be remembered that during this period the shopkeeper continued usually to live over his business premises, until the time came when he could no longer afford to do so—a time which coincided with the rise and development of the suburbs as we know them. The merchant who had his town residence in one of the Bloomsbury Squares, generally possessed a villa close to London—

[1] Londinium Redivivum.
[2] I speak more fully of these places of amusement in a subsequent chapter.

at Clapham or Richmond, and often drove his curricle into Town when living in these then rural districts; while the stage and mail coaches frequently brought the less wealthy from the environs. These coaches had their special inns in whose yards they put up, a custom brought vividly before us in the pages of Dickens and other contemporary writers.

Another form of amusement was provided by the coffee houses, where men not only refreshed themselves materially, but also read the papers, played cards and cribbage, etc., and which were used much as the regular clubs were by a higher strata of society.

The clubs proper were then limited in number, and Leigh's list contains but eleven. Of these the Albion, Arthur's, Boodle's, Brooks's, the Cocoa Tree, the General Service Club, Royal Guards, and White's, were in St. James's Street; the Alfred and the United Service were in Albemarle Street, and the Union in St. James's Square. Those that still exist and have changed their venue since 1818—the date of this list—are the Union which went to its present home in 1822, and the United Service which migrated to Pall Mall in 1826, to premises built by Nash.

The clubs may be said to have been the focus of much of the west end life of the period, but, except in one particular, they can hardly be regarded as centres of amusement. This was provided in a variety of ways, the chief temple being Almack's which, under its female oligarchy, flourished in a surprisingly successful manner, till it ceased to exist in 1863. Concerning the clubs where gambling had its headquarters, especially at Crockfords which opened its palatial house in 1827, and Almack's where etiquette enjoyed a stronghold it never secured elsewhere, and the dance flourished in new phases—the waltz, one of the most criticised and discussed, and the Quadrille—I shall have more to say in subsequent chapters. Here, in a sort of bird's-eye survey of the life of the period, I can but confine myself to generalities.

The man of fashion found his time fully occupied if he was one of the Dandies, in dressing and exhibiting himself in the streets or in the famous Bay Window of White's; or, if he was of a more sporting turn, in driving coaches and curricles; in patronising prize-fights; in riding in the Park, or loitering in St. James's Street or Bond Street. In the evening he attended the Opera or put in an appearance at a crush or "drum" as they began to be called; later he might be seen in some of those haunts which Pierce Egan, and " Blackmantle," and other contemporary observers of manners and customs, have perpetuated in their allusive, rather than strictly descriptive, pages. The doings of Tom and Jerry and the Oxonian may be highly coloured, as are the illustrations with which the Cruikshanks embellished these books of weird and wondrous records, but they possess a substratum of fact, and give, perhaps better than any other chronicle, a picture of the habits of the man about town of that full and boisterous time.

Curiously enough each phase of this sort of life seems to have produced an outstanding example. Thus we associate equestrianism with Lord Petersham, and driving with " Tommy " Onslow and Sir John Lade ; dress with Brummell and later with D'Orsay ; gastronomy with Lord Sefton, and wit with Luttrell and Sidney Smith. There were, of course, plenty of other exponents of all these " arts " ; but these were the outstanding protagonists, and it is around these that much of the gossip of the day centres.

Society, as we understand the term, was then very restricted. The phrase " The Upper Ten Thousand " at that time really possessed some measure of accuracy, although during the earlier years of the period the select might have been numbered much less amply. Almack's, as I have said, was a sort of testing ground, and the difficulty of penetrating that Elysium was extraordinary. Contemporary literature is full of references to the intrigues carried on, and the subterfuges resorted to, in order to gain a footing within its walls. The Princess Lieven, Lady Jersey, and Mrs. Burrell, were among the most prominent of the Lady Patronesses, as they were called, and even the great Duke had on occasion to bow before their dictates. Novels were written on the theme, and, according to the letters and diaries of the day, as many prayers were offered up and as much self-denial was undergone to get to Almack's as (not to say it profanely) to get to Heaven.

There were three other outstanding centres of fashionable life in London at this era. First there was Carlton House (before George IV commissioned Nash to reconstruct Buckingham House) where the First Gentleman, as Prince of Wales and as Regent, surrounded himself with those who pandered to his tastes or amused his blasé hours, until as King he withdrew to Windsor and was as little seen as the grand Turk. Then there was Holland House where from 1799 to 1840, there was hardly a distinguished person in all walks of life who had not been a guest, and whose annals have been written by Princess Liechtenstein, and whose archives have since been so admirably drawn upon by Mary, Lady Ilchester and the present holder of the title. And then there was Gore House in whose rooms from 1836 to 1849, Lady Blessington and Count D'Orsay received all the male notabilities of the day and a few of the great ladies.

Those who might have been seen during the day-time riding or driving in Hyde Park,[1] which had superseded St. James's Park— so fashionable in the 18th century—as a place of recreation, would meet in the evening at one of these three social centres.

Although the glory of Holland House just overlapped the beginning of the Victorian era, and Gore House proved an attraction for a dozen years after the young Queen had ascended the throne, there was evidence of a gradual change in Society just as there was in the life of the people. The oriental seclusion of George IV's last years was succeeded by the free and easy manners of his sailor brother who was accustomed (to Greville's horror) to wander about the streets and, in his way, to try and emulate the citizen-kingship of Louis Philippe. A train of soberer thought and a more correct conception of sovereignty was inaugurated by Queen Victoria, who, under the eyes of Prince Albert, that excellent, well-meaning, well educated, but somewhat stiff and formal consort, sternly set her face against all licence, and in the effort to counteract the bad effects of her two predecessors exhibited a tendency to go to the other extreme. The consequence was that the brilliancy of Carlton House was effaced by the drab monotony of Buckingham Palace, and although there were plenty of exceptions, and many people continued for a time to live a life that recalled the more spacious days of the Regency, as a whole the influence of the Court became paramount and London life proportionately less coloured and amusing

I say less coloured advisedly, because the phrase can be taken actually as well as metaphorically. The dress of the new reign reflected the dominant note,[2] and fashion books will show that a

[1] As examples of how customs have changed, one may quote Sir Algernon West who writes in his " Reminiscences " that no lady would, then, have willingly driven down St. James's Street or have dreamed of stopping at a club door. No lady of fashion went out to dinner except in a chariot, or entered a single horse carriage, till Brougham invented the vehicle named after him.

[2] An exception should be made in the case of the Twopenny Postmen, who used to go their rounds, with a bell and bag to collect letters and who were dressed in blue coats with red facings. By the bye, franking remained in use till the institution of Penny Postage in 1840.

sort of recrudescence of the puritan convention came over modes as it did over manners. We have never quite succeeded in throwing off that now far away influence, and in spite of jazzes and tangoes, in spite of the annual invasion of French fashions, we are still, at least in our dress, labouring painfully under the tremendous authority of the great Queen.

During the period under consideration there occurred a variety of circumstances which excited or depressed the London of that day. Its earlier years were marked by such epoch-making events as the union between Great Britain and Ireland; and the war with Napoleon, closing as to one epoch with Trafalgar and as to another with Waterloo, victories which resulted in public rejoicings of an outstanding character; such events, too, as the death of the Princess Charlotte in 1817, and the so-called Manchester Massacre of 1819; the death of George IV, and the Cato Street Conspiracy in the following year; the formation of the first railway in 1824, and the construction of the Thames Tunnel; the fight over the Catholic Emancipation in 1829, and the passing of the Reform Bill in 1832; the abolition of the Corn Laws in 1846, and the great financial panic in the tragic year of 1848, when the Chartists exerted their power, together with the sudden death of Sir Robert Peel (in 1850),[1] thrown from his horse in Constitution Hill, where the young Queen had been shot at in 1840 and again in 1848, all helped to mark this period as one of energy and unrest hitherto hardly paralleled in our annals.

The constant excitement aroused by the arrival of news from the front whether that front was on the sea, in the Peninsula or in Belgium, told on the people of London, and the interest, often enough the pain, with which the bulletins were perused, is well depicted in Wilkie's well-known picture. Then, too, victory was celebrated in the capital by displays of fireworks which, according to extant prints, were frequently on an extraordinarily elaborate scale. Such causes as these were responsible for what may be termed unusual stimulation of national interest. Others which had this character were such events as the trial of Queen Caroline, the visit of the Allied Sovereigns in 1814 (Plate 79), when Prince Blücher got so unmercifully mobbed in the streets; the great

[1] He died a few days later (July 2nd) in great agony. Chloroform had been discovered in this very year, but owing to its full uses not being recognised Peel was unable to benefit from what is undoubtedly the greatest discovery of any age.

One of the Advantages of Oil over Gas

"LONDON NUISANCES"
One of the Advantages of Gas over Oil
By R. Dighton

View down Regent Street from Piccadilly

From a Contemporary Print

Town Houses of the Regency Period
in Tavistock Square, Bloomsbury (1809)

PLATE 9

Interiors in the Regency Style, at
11, Montague Place, W.

Frost of the same year, when the Thames was frozen and fairs held on its unaccustomed surface; the overflowing of the river—then innocent of embankments—two years earlier; and a hundred other circumstances which happened fortuitously, and of which the citizen was not slow to make the most, either in the way of obtaining money or amusement or both.

The Londoner has always been attracted by crime and its detection and punishment, and the annals of Newgate during this period afford us many glimpses into the seamy side of urban life. The executions were then public sights, and Newgate and its purlieus were as much the centre of morbid curiosity as Tyburn had been during the preceding century. Whether it was Holloway and Haggerty paying the last penalty on February 22nd, 1807, for the murder of Mr. Steele on Hounslow Heath, or Thistlewood and others being executed for their share in the Cato Street Conspiracy of 1820, the crowds that surged round the Old Bailey were brought together by the chance of excitement, just as the Pillory, which was used till 1830, when Peter James Bosey was the last to undergo this ordeal, attracted its interested spectators. The Pillory stood at various spots: the Royal Exchange, the Old Bailey, Temple Bar, Lincoln's Inn Fields, Charing Cross, New Palace Yard, and Tyburn; and around these areas many disorderly scenes took place.[1]

It was formerly the custom to execute criminals near the scene of their crimes, and about the last to undergo punishment in this way was a sailor named Coleman, who was hanged in Skinner Street in 1807, opposite the shop of a Mr. Beckwith, which he had, with others, broken into and plundered. The executions at Newgate were public and Dickens and others, who raised their voices against the practice, have left on record their experiences of the degrading and revolting scenes which were witnessed on these occasions.

Although so many ameliorations gradually took place as regards public morals and manners during the first half of the century, its earlier years did not give very marked evidence of this, and one is surprised to find so many barbaric customs lingering on, in certain sections of the community, almost down to a time within the hazy remembrance of ancient people surviving till within a few years ago. Highway robberies were frequent, and footpads were to be met with

[1] In 1810 no fewer than six people were placed in a pillory at the bottom of Norris Street, Haymarket. The stocks survived in various villages well into the 19th century; the last used, in 1816, are said to have been at Yarmouth.

in parts of the city which are now fashionably inhabited,[1] and where probably the most formidable opponent one is likely to encounter is the tax-collector.

Duelling, although the custom was gradually falling into abeyance, still survived, and during the first quarter of the century, some scores of such meetings are recorded, including the famous encounter between Lord Camelford and Mr. Best, in the grounds of Holland House; that between Sir Francis Burdett and Mr. Paull; and those wherein Lord Castlereagh and Canning, Sir Robert Peel and Daniel O'Connell, Cannning and Hobhouse, among many others, were antagonists.

As further examples of how old manners and customs died hard, one has only to remember that the Press-gang and Crimping, as it was called, for the Navy and even for the Army, remained in force during the earlier part of the century, and that the incredible hardships inflicted on children in cotton mills or on the wretched sweep's apprentices—climbing boys, they were termed, still existed as a disgrace reprobated by those who troubled themselves about the miserable condition of the lower classes; while in the country places such barbaric functions as the ducking stool, and whipping post, and the hanging in chains of the dead bodies of criminals, remained well into the new century.

That the chief scenes of a sustained roughness of manners were in country districts goes without saying. Contemporary newspapers and the literature and letters of the times teem with examples of this, but in certain well-defined ways London was not by any means exempt; and the development of dress down to the end of George IVth's rule and the marked elegance of manners in a certain restricted area of Society only made the survival of less urbane customs, among other classes of the citizens, more marked and noticeable.

The period was a notable one, for it witnessed extraordinary progress in all sorts of directions. Science made strides which have been equalled only in recent days: Sir David Brewster, Faraday, Herschel, Owen, Darwin, Huxley, Murchison, Dalton, Lyell, and the rest were labouring in this inexhaustible field; the first iron ship

[1] An uncle of the writer who died in 1918, aged 96, remembered as a boy going to school through market-gardens and open fields, and being attacked by a footpad from whom he ran away, at a spot now covered by the large houses of South Kensington. His people lived in Battersea, then boasting but a few important houses, and little dreaming of its present closely packed assemblage of small dwellings.

was built, the first telegraph was constructed, photography came into being, and penny postage, to mention but these ; while the land became covered with iron rails—the hand-maids of progress and civilization, and Hudson, the railway king, enjoyed his short career of sovereign-like power and prosperity.

In the realms of literature the period was one of outstanding importance. The names of its greatest exponents are household words. Cowper died in 1800, Byron lived till 1824, Crabbe and Scott till 1832, Coleridge till 1834, and Wordsworth till 1850 ; Sheridan outlived the birth of Thackeray by five, and that of Dickens by six, years ; Charles Kingsley and Ruskin were born in 1819 (the year of Queen Victoria's birth), Froude a year earlier, Tennyson in 1809, Browning in 1812, Matthew Arnold in 1822. Appropriately, too, as it seems, the great school of female writers sprang up— successors to the Burneys and Austens of an earlier day— and under the first female sovereign since Anne we can note the names of Maria Edgworth, the Brontés, Mrs. Gaskell, " George Eliot," Mrs. Oliphant, Christina Rossetti and Jean Ingelow among the more prominent in a galaxy of female genius.

In the region of art—especially in that of landscape painting— the period was equally rich. Romney died in 1802, but Lawrence survived till 1837, while the dates of a greater than either, Raeburn, are 1756-1823. Beyond these names one cannot say much for portrait painting during the first fifty years of the century ; but in landscape, and in certain other directions of artistic endeavour, the era was one of outstanding importance. Constable, Turner, David Cox, De Wint, Prout, Copley Fielding, the marvellous youth Bonington, were all doing their best work ; while Flaxman and Chantrey were giving life to marble, Wilkie was reproducing the habits and customs of those around him, and Blake was pictorially setting down his dreams of genius.

The stage produced some of its great figures. John Philip Kemble did not die till 1823, Mrs Siddons survived till 1831 and Edmund Kean till two years later. Charles Kean lived from 1811 to 1868, and Liston and Munden, with whom one cannot help associating the great name of Lamb (who died in 1834), were amusing Londoners into the thirties of the last century. This, too, was the great era of the dancer. Malibran, Taglioni, Cerito, and how many others (Thackeray could tell us), all conquered London by their incomparable grace of movement, as we are, to-day, held

LIFE IN REGENCY AND EARLY VICTORIAN TIMES

in subjection by Pavlova and Karsavina and the other beautiful creatures who speak with their feet and are eloquent in silent movement.

In addition to all these there are three figures which stand out, not exactly in the realms of high art, but who by their quickness of perception of the manners and customs, the fads and follies, of the day, have taken a place apart, and who may be said to have preached sermons through the medium of the brush, the pencil and the graver: George Cruikshank, Richard Doyle and John Leech. The methods of all these men were as dissimilar as could be; but they all set out to portray the life of the London which they knew as they knew their own hands, and in their work we get, I think, as good an idea, an equally meticulous rendering, of the habits and dress of the Londoner of the earlier 19th century, as Hogarth gave us in his great output of an earlier day, combined with a gentle, urbane, satire which the boisterous Rowlandson and the savage Gillray,[1] hardly, if ever, attained.

II.—"STUCCO AND PAINT"

ALTHOUGH it is impossible to connect a change in the outward appearance of any great city with a specific date, we are at least able to associate fresh developments in architectural activity with certain outstanding periods: thus when we speak of the Elizabethan style or the Georgian, it is not to be assumed that we are actually confining ourselves to the reign of the "Fair Virgin thròned in the West," on the one hand, or to the reigns of the Georges on the other; for much so-called Elizabethan architecture and furniture probably dates from a slightly earlier or later period than that covered by her reign; and we are liable rather loosely to set down as Georgian, designs which had their genesis in the time of Anne at the one end of the era or in that of William IV at the other. Much the same may be said of the Regency and of earlier Victorian days. It so happens, however, that coincident with the beginning of the 19th century a very marked change did come over architecture as well as over manners and customs (Plates 8, 9, & 10), and this change is recognised as being associated with the Regency,

[1] Gillray died in 1815, Rowlandson in 1827.

PLATE 11A

THE BUCK'S MORNING TOILET

A QUADRILLE AT ALMACK'S

A FORCED ENTRY BY BROKERS' MEN

FASHION AND FOLLY (1823)

By W. Heath

PLATE 12

THE SUBURBS: OLD BROMPTON ROAD IN 1822
By G. Scharf

BELGRAVIA: ST. PETER'S CHURCH, EATON SQUARE
By W. Waller

although the Regency really only began in 1811.[1] In the same way we are accustomed to speak glibly of "Early Victorian," as applied to anything from houses and their contents to dress and the customs of its wearers, which had its origin from the days before the Queen came to the throne, and which was in vogue long after the earlier years of her reign may be said to have ended.

This being so, we may, I think, legitimately regard the years from 1800 to 1850 as covering the two periods known to us as those of the Regency and the early Victorian. In many respects these two eras merged into one another. Here and there people were found carrying on past traditions when marked changes were taking place around them; art and literature continued, in various directions, to reflect the ideas and aspirations of an earlier day. But taken as a whole, the change that occurred in habits of thought, in style of dress, in outward manners and customs, with the accession of Queen Victoria, was so obvious that even contemporaries must have realised that they were passing through a complete and drastic change.

Thus the period under consideration is cut into two well-marked divisions: the first covering the time from the beginning of the new century to the year 1837; the second dating from the accession of Victoria to the year marking the half century (1850). These fifty years are crowded with incident, are fresh in development of all kinds, and for a variety of reasons, may be properly regarded as among the most pregnant in the whole course of our history: for they saw not only the rise and fall of the Napoleonic idea, which affected us then somewhat as we have been affected recently by what one may call the pseudo-Napoleonic idea, but they witnessed the end of an old régime and the beginning of a brighter and more significant, if not as decorative, conception of life; they saw the inauguration of all sorts of schemes—sometimes halting and tentative enough, but still moving in the right direction towards the betterment of life; they were associated with the inventive geniuses who overcame distance and annihilated space; they brought with them those other geniuses who raised literature to a height it had not attained for many years, resuscitating in its poets and novelists the great days of the Augustan era, and in the persons of Dickens and Thackeray challenging comparison with the age that had produced Fielding and wept over Sterne.

[1] The earlier Regency proposed by Pitt in 1788 was made unnecessary by George III's recovery.

LIFE IN REGENCY AND EARLY VICTORIAN TIMES

The London of the Regency shows in its dimensions, its buildings and its institutions, as well, of course, as in the habits and customs of its citizens, a very marked advance over the metropolis as it was during the first half of George III's long reign; for towards the close of the century architectural development had made many and important strides, and by the beginning of George IV's rule, Nash, who stands somewhat to the architectural achievement of this day as do the Adams to that of an earlier period, had produced many of those, then as they seemed, remarkable schemes which still survive here and there, but which are gradually disappearing before still mightier structures. We can, to-day, see something of the effect produced, in Regent Street where the splendid curve which breathes the very spirit of the later Georgian times, has still power to impress in spite of the huge erections that rampart it about (Plates 7 & 14). But it is not here that the atmosphere of the Regency seems most markedly to dwell. Every age in a city has its particular characteristic points: in Elizabethan London it is the Strand and Fleet Street and Southwark that we chiefly associate with the figures of that spacious day; in Caroline times it is Whitehall; in earlier Georgian days, the Mall and Piccadilly. In the days of the Regency the two thoroughfares *par excellence* were St. James's Street (Plate 31) and Bond Street.[1] As you pace them now, in spite of drastic changes especially noticeable in the latter, the period rises vividly before you. You see Brummell, with Jack Lee on his arm, being cut by the Prince; you see Sefton hurrying into White's, and Fox coming from his lodgings in Arlington Street to lose money at Brooks's; the Bardolphian nose as well as the eloquent eyes of Sheridan, light up the street of streets; Alvanley prances by on horseback and Luttrell cuts his jokes on foot; while Carlton House stands in juxta-position to the old palace, and seems to challenge, with its progressive characteristics, the passing grandeur of a more solemn period.

For, to tell the truth, the Regency, degenerate and reprehensible as it was in its example in so many respects, was yet an attempt to give human nature more play than it possessed under the palmy days of the Farmer King; and just as an earlier effort (under Charles II) had degenerated into unparalleled licence after the

---

[1] It was the fashion in Brummell's time to lounge in Bond Street between the hours of 2 and 4 in the afternoon.

"STUCCO AND PAINT"

stern puritanism of the Protectorate, so the influence of the Carlton House set may be said to have marked another extreme of easy-going *joie de vivre*. The beginning of the new century may be taken as a commencement of this tendency—a tendency which gradually developed into the sort of life described by Pierce Egan, when noblemen appeared before furious magistrates charged with being drunk and wrenching off door-knockers; when the wretched "Charlies" (the watchmen of the period) were unsafe even in their exiguous boxes; when Gillray depicted the doings of the illustrious in outrageous caricature; when cock-fighting and eccentric wagers occupied much of the leisure, not only of the *hoi polloi*, but of the *jeunesse dorée*, of that full-blooded time.

What the setting to all these doings looked like may be seen in the wealth of illustration that has come down to us. At this period two schools of topography flourished in a way they had never done previously. In the former we get reproductions of older buildings which had descended to the 19th century either in their entirety or in a more or less ruinous condition. Men like Grove and Astle and J. T. Smith and the rest, occupied themselves with recording such architectural remains as were either threatened with demolition or were actually in the hands of the house-breakers, or becoming victims of Time the most potent house-breaker of all. The latter class of topographers were engaged in showing by pencil and brush what was actually being erected in London about this period. They did not all work in the first decade of the 19th century, but those who have left the best memorials of the metropolis of that period, are those who produced their work a few years after George IVth had come to the throne; and in the labours of such draughtsmen as Thomas Herne Shepherd; Bigot (who worked for Tallis); Archer; Schnebbelie; Capon; and the rest, one obtains an excellent idea of what London looked like during the first half of the nineteenth century. That there was an architectural monotony about the new buildings erected at this period is obvious. If you examine such a volume as Elmes's "Metropolitan Improvements," the drawings for which were done by Shepherd, you will realise this. The classic convention had obtained undisputed sway. From Regent Street and Carlton House Terrace (which effaced the Regent's Carlton House) to the Regent's Park and Charing Cross; from the Surrey Theatre to Drury Lane and Covent Garden; in Hoxton, where the Haberdashers' Almshouses had been rebuilt, to Highbury, where the College had been recently erected ; from the Duke of Westminster's (he was Lord Grosvenor then) new gallery attached to his house in Park Lane, to the Corn Exchange in Mark Lane or the London Orphan Asylum at Clapton, everything was on the classic model, cold and correct, but of that pattern-book style which cries aloud to be liberated from the spirit of servile imitation and seeks pathetically for some ray of originality and freedom from an earlier standard of architectural taste.

With regard to ecclesiastical design, there were two schools : one still clung desperately to the classics as may be seen in such embodiments as the New Church in Camden Town ; that in Regent Square ; the Catholic Chapel, Finsbury ; Trinity Church, in the New Road ; St. Peter's, Eaton Square (Plate 12), and many another. The Inwoods were responsible for many of these temples, as they may truly be termed ; J. S. Repton produced a similar sort of erection, in St. Philip's Chapel, Regent Street, built in 1819 but since demolished. But, it was Nash's influence that dominated them ; and inasmuch as some of these were in juxta-position to that architect's buildings it was necessity as much as taste that was responsible for their taking this particular form.

On the other hand Gothic was in the air. Barry came as a sort of counter-blast to Nash, and thus we find the National Scotch Church in Gray's Inn Road ; Trinity Chapel, Cloudesley Square ; St. John's Church, Holloway, and St. Luke's, Chelsea (to mention but these), conforming to this style, a style which was re-introduced into England through the influence of Horace Walpole in the foregoing century and which reached its climax under the hands of Pugin.

The ever increasing growth of the suburbs made many new churches necessary, and in 1818 an act—called the Million Act—was passed which resulted in the erection of forty or fifty places of worship. Most of them were in the classic style, but at least sixteen conformed to the Pointed Gothic convention ; although the true Gothic revival reached its apogée at a later period. Among the churches erected between 1820 and 1830, may be mentioned St. George's, Camberwell ; Holy Trinity, Southwark ; St. John's Waterloo Road ; Hanover Chapel, Regent Street ; St. Mark's, North Audley Street ; St. Peter's, Eaton Square ; St. Pancras, which cost £76,000 and has been described as " a mass of heathenism " ;

"STUCCO AND PAINT"

St. Peter's, Regent Square; All Souls', Langham Place; St. Philip's, Regent Street; St. Mark's, Kennington; as well as Sir Robert Smirkes' three churches: St. Mary's, Wyndham Place; St. Anne's, Wandsworth; and West Hackney Church. Contemporary representations of these edifices show them, with their cold and classic exteriors and pepper-box steeples (what a falling off from Wren's and Gibbs's glorious successes in this direction), and seem to give point to Eastlake's words, "Who does not remember the grim respectability which pervaded, and in some cases still pervades, the modern town church of a certain type, with its big bleak portico, its portentous beadle, the muffin-capped charity boys. Enter and notice the tall neatly grained witness boxes and jury boxes in which the faithful are empanelled; the "three-decker" pulpit placed in the centre of the building, the lumbering gallery which is carried round three sides of the interior on iron railings; the wizen-faced pew-opener eager for stray shillings; the earnest penitent who is inspecting the inside of his hat; the patent warming apparatus; the velvet cushions which profane the altar; the hassocks which no one kneels on; the poor box which is always empty."[1] (Plate 16). This might be from a page of Dickens, say in "Dombey & Son" where Mrs. Miff, the pew-opener, and Mr. Sownds, the beadle, hover round the company at Dombey's wedding, and sit on the steps and count their gains after the ceremony; or from a chapter—say that on some City Churches—in the "Uncommercial Traveller."

The Gothic Revival was practically contemporary with the Tractarian movement of 1833-41, and with it came into being those churches which Pugin and the rest designed: St. Luke's, Chelsea, the work of Savage, 1820-24, and a very successful one; St. Michael's, Highgate, for which Lewis Vulliamy was responsible in 1830-2; St. Dunstan's-in-the-West, with its beautiful tower, designed by James Shaw in 1831-3; Christ Church, Westminster, the work of Ambrose Poynter, in the early pointed style, which for so long possessed an unfinished tower; St. George's, Lambeth, another of Pugin's churches, designed in 1840; and St. Paul's Knightsbridge, completed by Cundy in 1843; to mention but these.

The year 1850 was one of great ecclesiastical activity, not only in church architecture, but also in a new and developed form of church ritual; and it closes a period which opened indifferently,

[1] "History of the Gothic Revival."

but during which the foundations were laid for a complete revolution in such matters.

Taken by and large, the London of the Regency and the earlier years of Queen Victoria's reign, while possessing many of the ancient features which have, to-day, disappeared, such as Temple Bar and the old Houses of Parliament ; the Sovereign's Entrance to the House of Lords (for which Soane was responsible in 1824), and other structures which the reader will easily call to mind as having been removed in our own time, was in its architecture cold and formal in that portion at least—the West-end particularly—where re-building had been rampant, or in those outlying districts where new churches or semi-official edifices had been set up.

The outlines of the London of this period may be traced best in Horwood's great plan, published about the beginning of the century and forming the first really systematic attempt to indicate, not only every street, but every house in the city. A smaller but equally convenient means of estimating the difference between the boundaries of London then as compared with what they are now, is afforded by Luffman's map, dated 1816. One can at a glance see by the sparsely covered areas of Pentonville and Islington, Hackney and Bethnal Green, and other then outlying portions of the metropolis, on the north side of the river, and Newington Butts, Kennington, Bermondsey, etc., on the south, what enormous strides have been made in building up London to its present immense proportions, in the century which has elapsed since Horwood and Luffman drew up their respective plans. Marked as are the changes in the parts here specified, it is in the West-end that they will be still more obvious to the reader. For instance, during the first quarter of the century there was no Belgravia, and east of Sloane Street as far as the backs of the old houses in Grosvenor Place, were the Five Fields crossed by a private road which connected Lower Grosvenor Place with the so-called Bloody Bridge at Sloane Square. Hans Place, with a collocation of houses and streets to its north, connecting it with Queen's Row and Brompton Row (now the Brompton Road), stood in the midst of open ground over which the backs of the houses on the west side of Sloane Street looked (Plate 12). All this district was called Hans Town, and in 1816 a small cricket ground, with Marlborough Gardens adjoining, seems to promise the presence of that famous Prince's Club which came into being in the seventies, and whose site Cadogan

View of Chelsea Embankment from the Old Church (1841)

By W. Parrott

PLATE 13

PLATE 14

VIEW DOWN REGENT STREET, LOOKING TOWARDS THE QUADRANT (1842)
By T. S. Boys

THE MANSION HOUSE, AND A VIEW DOWN CHEAPSIDE (1842)
By T. S. Boys

The Burning of the Old Houses of Parliament in 1835
From a Contemporary Print

Charing Cross, with a View of Northumberland House (1842)
By T. S. Boys

A Fashionable Preacher at
St. Margaret's, Westminster (1809)
By *Rowlandson & Pugin*

A Fashionable Wedding at
St. George's, Hanover Square (1841)
By *T. H. Shepherd*

PLATE 16

"STUCCO AND PAINT"

Square and its adjoining streets and houses now occupy. Cadogan Place was in existence, "the connecting link between the aristocratic pavements of Belgrave Square and the barbarism of Chelsea" as Dickens describes it in Nicholas Nickleby,[1] but between it and Sloane Street the ground, now occupied by the gardens attached to its houses, was then the "Botanic Gardens," which a Mr. Salisbury of Brompton had, in 1807, obtained in order to lay it out "with easy access to the public." The "barbaric" Chelsea then little dreamed of its present full and picturesque life. Picturesque it certainly was in its few old buildings where the beautiful Paradise Row and other features gave it a remote and old-world air (Plate 13); but it was little built over, and indeed east of the Hospital, then Tothill Fields, as far as Horseferry Road was open ground; although Luffman marks a "new road" extending from Brewer Street to Vauxhall Bridge, and an "intended" thoroughfare connecting Grosvenor Place with a point close to the southern termination of the new road. On the river side there is shown the "new Ranelagh" standing amid the "Neat Houses." But gardens and fields occupy all the area now closely covered with streets and buildings; while so little inhabited was anything west of the Barracks in Knightsbridge or Paradise Row, further south, that Luffman does not include what is now South Kensington and its vast westward stretching tentacles, within his plan. Indeed, except for an old house here and there, and a few smaller tenements, all this part was then given over to market gardens, and its creation as a residential area dates from a period later than the first half of the 19th century. This can be seen clearly from Mogg's plan of 1808[2], where all this large area is shown wholly undeveloped, as is also that other vast tract of ground now covered by houses and streets and generally known as the Westbourne (Mogg spells it Westbourn) district, and Tyburnia.

Thus we shall find that the London of the first few years of the 19th century, apart from outlying districts where buildings, sometimes quite important ones, stood, was really bounded on the west by Park Lane and the Edgware Road, on the east by a line running more or less due north from the Docks; on the north by the Maryle-

[1] Belgrave Square was formed in 1825 from the designs of Basevi—the large houses at the corners being the work of Philip Hardwick and others. The development was carried out by Cubitt.

[2] Heck's Plan dated 1851, also shows how little developed this area then was.

bone Road (then called the road to Paddington) and the City Road, on the south—disregarding the river as a boundary—by what are now the New Kent Road and St. George's Road. Paddington was then a village with its church and green and a few houses around them, reached from the Metropolis by the Edgware Road; Pentonville, Islington and Camden Town were but arms thrown out from the main body; Hackney, Bow and Stepney were in similar case; while Surrey Square, on the Kent Road, marked practically the end of building development in this quarter, Camberwell being a rural village and the Oval standing among fields. In 1808 there was no bridge at Vauxhall; it came three years later, although as Mogg marks its outlines tentatively, it had by then been obviously arranged for. Ranelagh had been closed in 1803, but Vauxhall was to have still a long lease of life, and it is shown, by Mogg, with some particularity, its formal paths and alleys being clearly indicated. Although the Regent's Park was yet to come, there seems to have been some anticipation of it in a " Proposed British Circus $1\frac{1}{4}$ miles in circumference, pleasure grounds 42 acres," which is tentatively marked as to be situated just west of Primrose Hill—an eminence which then stood out in the country with no buildings near it but the rural St. John's Wood Farm, Chalk Farm, and the more remote fastenesses of Highgate and Hampstead.

From a comparison of Mogg's plan and that of Carey dated 1792, we shall see that during the sixteen years that elapsed between their appearance, no very important developments had taken place in the outlying portions of London. But if we place the former beside that (say) of Fores, issued in 1835, the changes will be found to be of the most far-reaching description. Belgravia has come into existence; the Regent's Park, with its ramparts of Nash's houses and terraces, has been formed; Stepney and Bethnal Green have become covered with streets and dwellings; the areas north of the Marylebone and Euston Roads have been developed; and the vast district south of the Thames, has grown to such an extent as to threaten the rural characteristics of Camberwell and even to stretch towards Peckham and Dulwich. Seven years later the changes are still more pronounced, and by the aid of Bauerkeller's embossed map, published by Ackermann in 1842, we shall see what London looked like practically at the close of the first half of the century. During the years that elapsed between the issue of Horwood's plan and that of Bauerkeller, many new buildings were erected, much development took place,

"STUCCO AND PAINT"

and in the latter we have essentially the London as it emerged from its tentative beginnings in 1800. The total number of its population is then given as 1,800,000[1] odd, a figure that is sufficient in itself to shew what enormous strides the city has made in development during the last seventy years. So much, I think, is all that it is necessary to say on this point. A close examination of the plans specially mentioned here, as well as innumerable others, will shew many curious changes, but here these can only be indicated in a general way. Bauerkeller states that the city in 1842 extended some seven and a half miles in length and about five miles in breadth; in 1808 Mogg's measurements are roughly five miles by three and a half!

Before we have quite done with maps I should like to say a word about the great plan of London, which R. Horwood issued in 1794 and again in 1799. This remarkable achievement, which is to our period what that of Rocque was to an earlier day, shows every dwelling in the Metropolis, and, what is of particular value for a variety of reasons, gives the number then in use on each house; besides, of course, accurately marking the divisions of the various parishes and other points of interest and importance. Its scale is such that the correct outlines of the more outstanding features can be set down; thus to take an instance or two, we see the circle of Tattersall's[2] old premises behind St. George's Hospital, before Grosvenor Crescent was dreamed of; as well as the old Knightsbridge Barracks lower down on the same side of the road; while the ground plan (for it is actually that) of Buckingham Palace, indicates clearly the alignment of that building when it was called Buckingham House, and was innocent of the eastern facade, which Blore added to it.

So much for the outlines of the London of 1800-1850. What, it may be asked, were the changes that occurred in the actual bricks and mortar which made up, so to speak, the city of this period. Well, as in all plays (and London life, then particularly, afforded material for dramas of many kinds) the scenes change. First we get

---

[1] The population of London during the first half of the 19th century has been estimated as follows: 1801, 888,198; 1811, 1,013,008; 1821, 1,234,338; 1831, 1,508,469; 1841, 1,693,081; 1850, 2,240,289. Well might M. Léon remark, "Londres n'est plus une ville; c'est une province couverte de maisons."

[2] Salwey's coloured plan of the high road from Hyde Park Corner to the west, issued in 1811, gives a still clearer indication of this particular part of London.

the later Georgian bricks and mortar as they come down to us, in the houses that were erected in the earlier portion of the 18th century ; what we may term the Mayfair convention ; as well, of course, as various relics of an earlier period, gradually falling into decay as many of these were. Then, we have dwellings in the later Georgian style—we may term them the Bloomsbury group—the houses which the Osbornes and the Sedleys and such like types of the rich merchant class affected (Plate 8). Anon, between 1810 and 1820, came Nash, with his pail of stucco, and transformed much of the West-end into the pale (I intend no paronomasia) monotony which has to some extent (as may be seen in South Kensington and Tyburnia to-day) still clung, limpet-like, to the dwellings of those who, to use Henley's phrase " go down to the west in broughams." Blore and Cundy and the Inwoods carried on, or contemporaneously associated themselves with, this tradition, a tradition which, while defensible in itself, cannot be said, in a climate loaded with dirt such as we experience in London, to be wholly for the best, unless, indeed, we regard it from the view of the house painter.[1]

The covering up of honest brickwork by this rather meretricious style of decoration, has something in it, I think, not wholly foreign to the factitious life of the earlier part of our period ; and that it should have arisen and flourished during the Regency shows how the manners and customs of the day influenced architectural development. The point need not be laboured. There it is, and the fact remains that there was a tendency to give a false and somewhat unreal air to the brickwork that under Leverton and Brettingham and others has remained a joy to us to-day because of its intrinsic excellence and the mellowness with which it clothes London. There is no monotony in a row of matured red brick houses, as may be proved by innumerable instances in Mayfair and Bloomsbury alone ; but Carlton House Terrace and even Regent Street (saved as it is by its glorious curve) strike a note of sameness even if that sameness be one associated with rich and opulent existence.

Contemporary topographical draughtsmanship has a particular bearing on the Metropolis of the period, for without it we should have but a hazy idea of the appearance of the streets of London and

---

[1] A reference to Messrs. Richardson and Gills' valuable work, "London Houses from 1660 to 1820" (Batsford), will enable the reader to discover the actual dates when prominent residences were erected, in St. James's Square in 1800, for instance, and in Carlton House Terrace in 1829.

the life that surged amid them. The London of the 18th century becomes an actuality to us largely through the pictorial efforts of such men as Canaletto and Scott, Dayes, Bowles, Sandby, Rooker, and many another. The city as our forebears knew it at a later date is no less equally familiar to us through the work of Archer and Shepherd, J.T. Smith, and, above all, Thomas Shotter Boys, in whose beautiful pictures we have not only works of art of the first importance (was he not a pupil of Bonington, and did he not follow his great master closely and faithfully), but we have representations of buildings and the general aspect of streets, of costumes and conveyances, and the thousand and one items that make a mere topographical drawing a record of permanent value, set down with amazing fidelity, and sentient in every line with true and deep artistic feeling (Plates 14, 15, & 37).

There is another source from which we may learn much of the city as it appeared at the beginning of the reign of Victoria. Innumerable maps and plans we possess, as I have indicated, and Horwood's great effort was supplemented at various periods by the publications of such men as Mogg, Carey, Luffman, Bauerkeller and innumerable others. From these we can trace the alignment of the streets, and the relative state of development of the Metropolis as a whole. But it is not to these that I refer, but to the series of street views which Tallis issued from about 1838 onwards, and which reproduce the elevations of all the houses and shops to be found in the chief thoroughfares of the city. The growing rarity of these remarkable productions give them an attraction for collectors of "Londoniana." But regarded from a less restricted standpoint, they are documents of the greatest value and importance, and we have only to consider what we should feel if something of the sort (say from the hand of Hollar) was suddenly discovered showing how London appeared during the reign of Charles I, to realise what will be the reception of these little views, say two hundred years hence.

CHAPTER II.

THE REIGN OF THE DANDIES

WE have seen, in the last chapter, something of what the stage and scenery were like in the London of the earlier years of the 19th century. Let us endeavour to obtain some insight into the play itself and the *dramatis personæ*. The action of the piece (to pursue the theatrical metaphor) will carry us into many different localities, and we shall find ourselves involved with many different characters—the statesman and the merchant, the prize-fighter and the wit, the poet and the gamester. But two types rise dominant above the rest and distinguish this period better than any other—the Dandy and the Wit. It is rather curious that this should be so, for taking it as a whole, the era can hardly be said to have been one that shone specially either in dress, as did the 18th century, or in the lambent play of brains, as did the later 17th. Perhaps the reason why the wits and dandies of this time form so outstanding a feature in London life, is because the mass of Londoners were not markedly endowed with wit, or capable of initiating or carrying off fashionable modes and fancies. Whatever the reason, the fact remains that the Regency is marked by the cut of a coat or the utterance of an epigram; and the pre-eminent figures are those of such men as Brummell, who was followed by D'Orsay, just as Luttrell was succeeded as a sayer of good things by Theodore Hook and Sydney Smith. The Dandy's epic has still to be written—but when it is, the protagonists will be these two men, dissimilar in capacity, in tastes, in ambition, but linked together as the most conspicuous professors of that great theory of clothes which a few years later the deep thinker of the day was to embody into something like a new philosophy.

The life of Brummell (Plates 18 & 19) has been frequently recorded;[1] his over-mastering personality dominates the fashionable life of the period until his downfall in 1816; he serves as the lay figure for innumerable discourses on all sorts of subjects, from the art of dress to the vanity of human wishes; and yet it is probable that his secret will never be wholly known. He was a mass of contradictions: he could be exquisitely polite and appallingly rude; at one moment acting

[1] Captain Jesse wrote the classic 'Life' of the Beau, which appeared in two volumes in 1844; De Monvel produced his "George IVme et George Brummell," in recent years, a book translated by Mrs. Craven; and Barbey D'Aurevilly's "Du Dandyism et de Georges Brummell," is famous.

GEORGE IV AS PRINCE REGENT
From the Painting by Sir Joshua Reynolds

THE DUKE OF YORK (LEFT) AND GEORGE IV
IN SILHOUETTE By Crosshurst of Brighton

BRUMMELL AS A YOUNG MAN
Engraved by J. Cooke from a Miniature

MRS. FITZHERBERT
From an Engraving after Cosway

PLATE 18

THE REIGN OF THE DANDIES

like a gentleman, at another like a barbarian; he said the stupidest things, but he also enunciated some very telling ones; he was often heartless, but now and again showed a curious sensibility; he was capable of inspiring deep and lasting friendships, but he alienated many an intimate; like Shakespeare he lost the world for a jest, and was content to lose it. Surfeited with such admiration and such power as no one else has ever attained in a similar direction, he seems on set purpose to have brought about a quarrel with the royal friend who, when all is said, was far less of a gentleman than the confectioner's grandson he patronised. In whatever way you look at him one must concede that Brummell was a great man— great in a circumscribed area of life, if you will, but still—great. For he set out with a determination to attain a certain position, and in spite of few advantages, beyond natural ease of manner, pleasant appearance (he was hardly to be termed good looking), and consummate impudence, he reached his goal. He was the Napoleon of fashionable life, and if the capture of Carlton House may be said to have been his Marengo, the famous " Who's your fat friend " was undoubtedly his Waterloo. Like his great prototype he died miserably in exile, but in his way he will be remembered as long as the marvellous Corsican.

Brummell's name is not only indissolubly linked up with the annals of fashion; his personality dominated for two decades that small but influential portion of London in which Carlton House and Almack's radiated a dual influence. We all know how circumscribed the actual topographical area of that little world was. Theodore Hook, it will be remembered, thought that that portion of St. James's, bounded by Piccadilly and Pall Mall, St. James's Streetand Waterloo Place, was the *ne plus ultra* of fashionable life, and his dictum, exaggerated as are most generalities, did contain a modicum of truth in those days, and is besides interesting as showing how restricted was the kingdom which Brummell ruled. For it is a fact that the great Dandy is associated with very few parts of London outside this district. True, he once adventured as far as Charing Cross where Sheridan met him and received apologies from the beau for being so far east; and on one famous occasion he attended a ball given by a Mrs. Thomson in the neighbourhood of Finsbury, but these were exceptions proving the rule; and Brummell's haunts were the streets of fashion immediately around Hook's selected centre.

LIFE IN REGENCY AND EARLY VICTORIAN TIMES

Brummell lived at various houses in London, of which 4, Chesterfield Street[1] is the best known (why is there no tablet commemorating the fact?—epic in its way); he passed thence to St. James's Street, to White's and his other clubs, Watier's for instance, which stood on the site of 81, Piccadilly and of which he had been one of the founders. It was in St. James's Street that he turned the tables so successfully on the Prince who cut him there; it was at Carlton House that he told his royal host to ring the bell[2]; it was in his earlier, less sophisticated days that he visited his aunt, Mrs. Searle, at her little farm in the Green Park, opposite Clarges Street, and there first met the Prince who was destined to be both his good and his evil genius. All this portion of the London of those days is as closely associated with Brummell as Kensington Gore and Hyde Park were to be, at a later period, with his one really notable successor, D'Orsay.

But although Brummell was the sun in this fashionable firmament, he was surrounded by many minor constellations which reflected and acted as a foil to his glory. There was Lord Alvanley, who had succeeded Selwyn as a wit and almost rivalled Brummell as a dandy; there was "Teapot" Crawfurd and "Ball" Hughes, "Poodle" Byng and Jack Lee, "King" Allen and Lord Petersham, Sir Lumley Skeffington and Scrope Davies, a wit of no inconsiderable merit, but whose name is chiefly remembered as being associated with Brummell's exit from the world he had ruled for so many years. In the pleasant garrulous pages of Gronow you may read of the sayings and doings of these super-men of fashionable London life. How they dressed; how they gambled; what they said; their failings; their meannesses; often their unbounded generosity, are all set down with meticulous care by one who lived among them, and was of them. And just as Gronow has recorded all their habits of life and manners of speech, so has Dighton left us a gallery of portraits where you can see the " hump " of Lord Sefton—that *bon vivant* who gave his famous dinners at 21, Arlington Street, under the superintendence of the great Ude; the top boots and gaiters of " Poodle " Byng (Plate 19); Lord Manners with his " Caniche "

---

[1] In 1799 he was here; in 1800 at 95 Park Street, Grosvenor Square; in 1801, in Upper Grosvenor Street; and later, between 1803 and 1809, at 18 Bruton Street and 24 South Street.

[2] It is known, of course, that there are various versions of these anecdotes to which allusive reference is here made; indeed, many of the stories concerning Brummell are clearly apocryphal, but there was a substratum of truth in most of them.

and the Duke of Devonshire with his cane ; Lord Allen with his hook nose, and "Kangaroo" Cooke, looking like a fashionable Blücher. All these, in their manner, as they lived, can be reconstructed, so to speak, by the aid of the draughtsman's pencil, and in his pictures we can see them as they were seen passing down St. James's Street, entering White's, loitering in Pall Mall, or killing the evening hours at Almack's, or in other less reputable haunts.

Most of these protagonists of fashionable life indirectly prove the influence of the man who stands in the forefront of their ranks, for to take an instance, it will be observed that nearly all of them wear trousers in place of the top-boots of a slightly earlier day and it will be remembered that among the enduring marks of Brummell's one time authority, was the reception given to this article of male attire which he had introduced from Germany during the days of his sartorial power.

Many of these men, who were far better born, richer, more influential in many walks of life, and far wittier than their leader, owed their position in fashionable life to him ; but the numbers of young men who were ruined by trying to follow his example and by aping his extravagance and impudence, are forgotten. An anecdote records one example, as when an indignant father remonstrated with the beau for leading his son astray, and received the reply : "Why, sir, I did all I could for him. I once gave him my arm all the way from White's to Brookes's." Then there was the beau's retort to another would-be butterfly who in order to get elected to one of the fashionable clubs, had advanced him a large sum of money, and one day hinted at repayment : " Your money," said Brummell, " I thought I had repaid it." "When ? " asked the astonished creditor. "When ? Why, the day before yesterday, when I was on the balcony of White's and saw you passing in the street and said Good-day, Jimmy, how are you ? ' ".

But stories such as these have been reiterated until they are known by heart. If they prove anything it is not exactly callousness but a conception of morals which was accepted by those who almost came to consider that a word of recognition cancelled a debt, and that a stroll down St. James's Street in Brummell's company was full payment for the loss of a fortune.

St. James's Street, Pall Mall and Bond Street have materially altered in outward appearance since that time ; but one can revivify these thoroughfares in the mind's eye as they were when the effulgent Prince strolled about them, or when Brummell and his band gave them that air of fashion which has never entirely deserted them, even in days when democratic influences are making themselves so markedly felt.

If you examine a print of St. James's Street as it was during the last two decades of George III's reign (Plate 31), you will be able to pick out certain prominent features which remain, and which then formed the background to the play of the Dandies: the old palace at its foot; Boodles, remaining as the Adams designed it; Brooks's, not materially changed from what it was; Lock's famous hat shop, less altered still. Fewer shops were there then, and, of course, the skyline has been altered out of all recognition by the erection of loftier buildings with more ambitious frontages. Bond Street has undergone changes almost as drastic. There is an interesting colour print showing that portion of it where Long's Hotel stood at the corner of Clifford Street, where Scott met Byron in 1815. The topographical part of this little picture is but a setting for the fashion-plate figures past which Lord Petersham rides on his bay. The dominant note of the streets then was colour. Except when in mourning, even the men seldom appeared in what at Oxford they call subfusc hues. A blue coat or a red waistcoat, a brown-furred paletot, or a yellow chesterfield, vied with the decorative uniforms of the military, or the kaleidoscope garments and wondrous head-dresses of the fair sex, whose charms of feature were hidden by enormous poke bonnets and whose ankles (how different is the case to-day!) were discreetly concealed by long skirts (Plate 38).

The years immediately succeeding the close of the Napoleonic struggle marked the apotheosis of extremes in dress and manners,[1] and many of the dandies, who, on Wellington's own showing, fought so bravely under his command, were among those who led the fashion of ultra-dress and ultra-amusements. The high priestesses of Almack's set a different fashion, that of rigid exclusiveness, and it is probable that at no period of our history were the lines of demarcation between the upper and the middle classes so stringently adhered to, although brains sometimes broke through these

[1] Many skits on fashionable life were published about this time—Luttrell's "Advice to Julia," and "Crockford House," Owen's "Fashionable Life Displayed," and some of Tom Moore's lesser lucubrations are among those that have survived, and may be turned over by the curious.

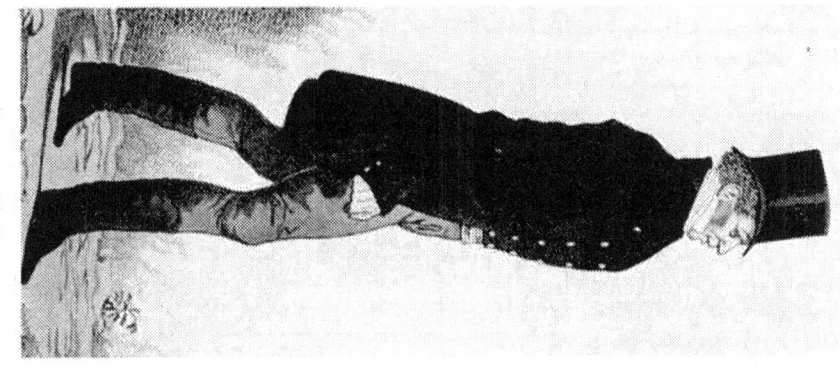

"Poodle" Byng
By R. Dighton

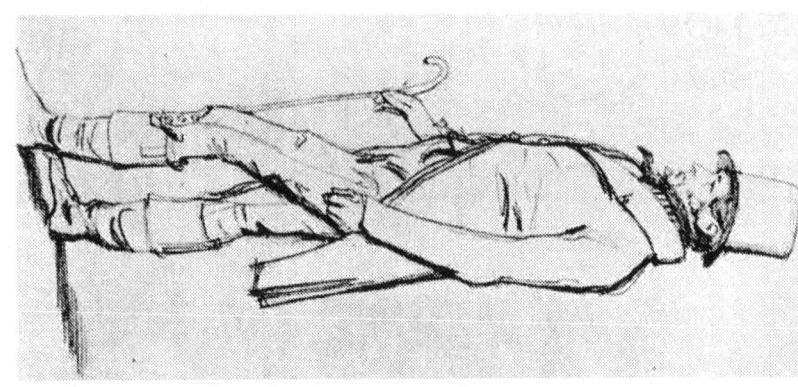

"Nimrod" (Mr. Apperley)
From a drawing by Maclise

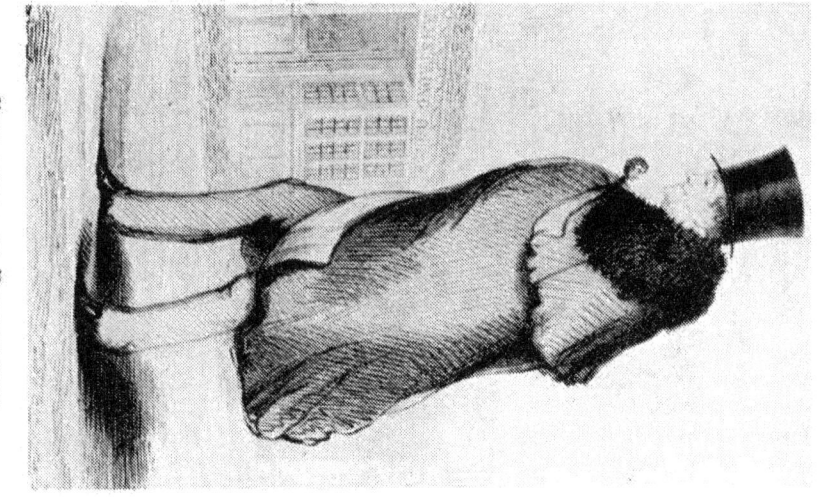

Brummell in Retirement
A contemporary Portrait

PLATE 29

THE BUCK KNOCKED SENSELESS BY A PASSING VEHICLE IS REVIVED IN AN APOTHECARY'S SHOP, WHILST A STREET CROWD GATHERS AT THE WINDOWS (1824)
From a Contemporary Print

THE DRUNKEN BUCK AND THE "CHARLEY"
From a Contemporary Engraving

artificial barriers, and the rise of the wits is almost contemporaneous with that of the dandies.

Many of the former were either men of aristocratic birth like Alvanley; connected with old families in a rather obscure way like Luttrell; or who, like Sidney Smith (Plate 45), had an entrance to society by the help of their special callings. They spent the best part of their time in the limited area to which, as we have seen, society confined itself. They lived in the streets about St. James's or Mayfair, they frequented the clubs, and the gambling hells which were to be found in the by-ways of the neighbourhood, they rode and drove in the Park, and when encountered further afield it was in the saloons of Holland House and Gore House in the west, or in the coulisses of Covent Garden, at Tom Cribb's, at a cock-fight in Westminster, or among the cadgers in the slums of what was called "The Holy Land" in the east.

The man of fashion occasionally, of course, paid visits in the country, to Belvoir or Badminton, Longleat or Arundel, but in those days difficulty of communication made such jaunts important and often arduous undertakings. Posting was, of course, the means of reaching such places; the coach being below the dignity of the dandy. When, however, "Tommy" Onslow and Sir John Lade made the driving of four-in-hands fashionable, these were to be seen carrying illustrious ones, not only to country houses, but to Bath, Tunbridge Wells and Brighton, all of which places enjoyed a vogue at this period, the last although was, on account of the Prince having cast an eye of favour upon it, the most patronised. The pavilion exists to show the sort of vitiated taste in architecture which pleased the royal mind, and the Old Steyne is still capable of conjuring up memories of the days when Mrs. Fitzherbert lived there like a queen, and when George Osborne and Emmy and Becky Sharp strolled about its precincts.

It is customary to think of the life of the dandies, or indeed of the leisured class generally, as being an empty and shallow sort of existence. The fact is that, in his way, the man of fashion, was as much and as fully employed as the merchant or the shop-keeper— only it was in a different direction. The commercial man went on 'Change, was occupied in his office or counting house, and gambled for money on the Stock Exchange, as the Dandy gambled at White's or Crockford's or passed his time in the business of dress, or of exhibiting himself—the finished article— in White's famous bay-window;

at Tattersall's (Plate 23), then at Hyde Park Corner, in the fencing rooms in St. James's Street; in the boxing saloon of "Gentleman" Jackson in Bond Street; or in his own apartments holding colloquy with his tailor, his bootmaker and his dog fancier, and the rest. When the merchant had retired to well-earned rest to his house in Bloomsbury or his villa at Clapham, the fine gentleman betook himself to Carlton House (if he was a friend of the Prince) or Almack's, or the drawing-rooms of great ladies, or passed exciting evenings throwing mains or playing whist. The point of view is everything; and there is no doubt that the man about Town fully occupied his time, and, if in a different way still as arduously as the man of affairs or the statesman.

The Turf was another outlet for the energies of certain members of this class, many a one of whom was a dandy *malgré lui*, whose tastes were not essentially those of the beau *par excellence*, but who, unless he was such a big man, as the "Jockey of Norfolk," that he could afford to dress badly, felt obliged to follow the lead of a Brummell or a D'Orsay in sartorial extravagances. Ascot and Epsom (Plates 41, 52, & 54), were then as popular as they have ever been; Banstead Downs saw its crowds congregated for a prize-fight (Plate 50), when pugilists like Jackson or Tom Sayers were protagonists in those Homeric struggles which Borrow was later to describe with such unction, and which so often form subsidiary pictures in the novels of our own day dealing with that period.[1]

But all these diversions, *extra muros*, as we may term them, were but incidents in the fashionable life of the time; and it is probable that not even in the preceding century was this sort of existence so confined to London, as it was in the years preceding the era when railways came into being and gradually helped to intermingle urban and country life, and to link up with the city hitherto wellnigh inaccessible spots.

Of all the extraordinary advances made by scientific discovery, there is none which so tended to alter the life of the country, as the introduction of the steam engine. The first railroad was opened in 1824, and although it was many years before the land became covered with iron rails, that event may be taken as inaugurating a new era—an era which had the most marked and far-reaching influence on London life (Plate 69). With it the days of posting

[1] George Meredith, Conan Doyle (cf. "Rodney Stone"), and Mr. Bernard Shaw, *inter multos alios*, have all given us life-like pictures of such scenes.

and the old coaches—although they lingered on in many places for considerable periods—may be said to have been numbered. It had, too, its influence on fashion. Hitherto the dress of the Londoner had something bucolic in it—the cut-away coat and top boots (Plate 19) gave their wearers an air as if they were always awaiting a stage coach or were prepared to post into the fastnesses of the country. With the coming of railways a gradually changed appearance overspread the form of dress, and darker hues began to prevail. It may be that one is confounding the effects with the wrong cause, but one cannot help noticing the significance of the change and connecting it with this scientific innovation.

If you look at the accompanying fashion-plate (Plate 24) you will observe what an alteration there is in dress and headgear. Whether the disappearance from the scene of George IV and the, by now, almost forgotten influence of Brummell, together with a sort of puritan revulsion (such as I indicated in Chapter I.) were alone responsible for this, I leave the philosopher to discover. Innovations are seldom the result of single causes; and so we may, I think, link up with these the coming of the iron horse, as determining factors in the change.

The dissemination of a limited sort of republicanism—a result of the French Revolution— may also have had something to do with this gradually increasing innovation. But although so marked a transformation came over fashion in this respect, especially in male fashion, the old styles lingered on tenaciously among certain people, and we know that when Dibden once breakfasted with Lord Erskine in 1802, he found his host attired in a dark green coat, a scarlet waistcoat, and silk breeches; and in the same year Mr. Pitt might have been seen perambulating the streets of Cambridge, wearing the cocked hat of an earlier day. Charles James Fox was another who affected the older style; while the Prince of Fashion constantly appeared in public wearing wonderful garments of striped green velvet, embroidered with silver flowers, and a powdered wig adorned with a profusion of curls, and finished off by a pigtail. Fashion often dies hard, especially when decorative effect is to be superseded by a more sombre note, and few things prove, I think, the supremacy which Brummell exerted, more than the fact that he was able to initiate and make popular among a certain set a dress which relied for its effect almost solely on the cut of the tailor and the manner with which it was carried off by the wearer.

LIFE IN REGENCY AND EARLY VICTORIAN TIMES

Wigs were in use down to the earlier years of the 19th century, and when discarded the hair was powdered, until Pitt saw an opportunity of increasing the revenue by a tax on this commodity, when the richer classes gave it up. Many, however, still paid their guinea—they were called " guinea pigs "—and in 1812 there were no fewer than 46,000 who did so. It is recorded that in Langport, in Somersetshire, every gentleman used powder, and an old Tory officer in Derby refused to send his son to a certain school there, in 1820, because the clerical master used no powder in his hair !

" The Cigar Divan," by George Cruikshank.

The rule of the Dandies continued in spite of the changes in dress which came about accompanied by an evolution in manners and ways of life ; but in place of Brummell and his set there arose D'Orsay, and his Crockford's took the place of Watier's, and for Carlton House there was Gore House (Plate 34) where Lady Blessington shared the honours with the Count, and where were to be met that galaxy of gorgeously-dressed young men so many of whom were as well furnished with brains as they were with clothes.

In the first place D'Orsay himself (Plate 25) was much more than a mere clothes-horse : he was a man of exquisite culture, an artist of no mean capacity, the friend of statesmen and the intimate of men whose names are illustrious in a dozen walks of life, and even Macready, a good but not a lenient judge, has left on record that D'Orsay was the most brilliant, graceful and endearing man he had ever met.

Although there were some of the old " Dandy " set represented at Gore House such, for instance, as " King " Allen and " Poodle " Byng, " Ball " Hughes and " Apollo " Raikes, the majority were new young men then entering on careers, many of which led to fame.

THE REIGN OF THE DANDIES

Here were to be seen Bulwer Lytton with his ambrosial curls, and Disraeli with his raven locks and wondrous waistcoats (Plate 35); Dickens, radiant in the glory of Pickwick's success, was among the dandies, and so was Thackeray; while if Hook and Sidney Smith, Luttrell and Rogers, Monckton Milnes and Bernal Osborne cannot strictly be classed in this category, they all more or less conformed to the prevailing modes of elaborate toilets, and were to be met in these crowded rooms where the great warrior of the age put in an occasional appearance, and the inscrutable eyes of the "Man of Destiny" watched a life that was somewhat alien to him.[1]

With the advent of Count D'Orsay into London life, the dandies of whom he was the acknowledged head, enlarged their outlook and justified their existence far more than they can be said to have done under the *régime* of Brummell. In the first place, connected as he was with Lady Blessington, a woman of wit, beauty and accomplishments of no mean order, D'Orsay associated with his development of the art of dress and style something more nearly approaching the conduct of a "salon" than has ever before or since been achieved in this country. As an artist and cultivated man generally, he had leanings towards what may be termed aristocratic bohemianism, that is to say he loved to surround himself by those who were eminent in all walks of life, irrespective of birth, provided they acted up to the high standard of bearing of which he was himself so shining an example, and so long as they conformed with that decorative sartorial ideal of which he was during a decade the most notable exponent. The consequence was that, with the exception of Holland House, there was no more brilliant or better dressed society to be found in London, from 1836 to 1849, than in Kensington Gore.

Another direction in which D'Orsay made his influence felt was in riding. He was himself a past master in the art of the *haute école*, who, when mounted on a high stepping horse, such as may be seen in Grant's well-known picture, attracted all eyes, which were as much riveted on his blue coat and gilt buttons, thrown back to show the wide expanse of snowy shirt front and buff waistcoat; his tight leathers and polished boots, his well curled whiskers, wide brimmed, glossy hats, and spotless white gloves,[2] as on the splendid animal he bestrode and the accomplished ease with which he

---

[1] See for a fuller account of Gore House and its habitués, the following chapter.
[2] Lord Lamington's description.

managed his mount. The consequence was that equestrianism became markedly popular, and the Park, as well as the high roads that led to Richmond and the other suburban resorts, were crowded with well-mounted men and women, as may be seen in the accompanying reproduction of one of Boys's beautiful lithographs (Plate 27); a phase of life to which the pencil of Leech was to give a further perpetuation, and the graver of Doyle a characteristically humorous, but no less suggestive, touch.

The fact is that, *pace* the sturdy Briton who thinks that all foreigners are lacking in the masculinity which he himself is supposed to possess in so large a degree, it was a foreigner who introduced a far more virile note into the life of the Dandy than Brummell had ever been able, or inclined, to do. The difference between these two leaders of elegance is perhaps most marked in this. But there were other points of difference; and even if the one combined with the other in exquisite taste in attire as well as in love of gambling, there the likeness ends. For D'Orsay was a splendid fellow in size and feature, Brummell was only impressive by dint of dress and manner (his bow was, of course, famous); D'Orsay was a brilliant all-round man—an artist, a sculptor, and well-read, who met on terms of equality most of the outstanding intellects of the day; Brummell was little else than a sharp, hard-headed young gentleman who knew how to impress by impudence and how to make impertinence pay. In short, the greater man was a gentleman among dandies, the lesser a dandy among gentlemen. Generalizations are often dangerous; but that seems to me to sum up the relative qualities of the two men who ruled London society during the first fifty years of the 19th century.

"The Last Look," by George Cruikshank.

The life of the citizen outside the magic circle of Almack's and the Dandies' influence, during the period, is a subject so large and complex that one can hardly hope to explore even the fringe of it in a short general survey; but at least a few of the more salient points may be noticed as being likely to serve as indications of the rest.

In the first place it must not be assumed that Society was wholly confined to the few hundreds which then constituted what the press was fond of calling the "Haut Ton." This restricted band did, indeed, influence a certain section of life in a more complete and drastic way than has ever since been the case. But there were plenty of people of good birth and good position who were outside its magic circle and were, surprisingly, quite contented to be. There were, of course, in many instances the same intrigues to gain admittance, the same unholy joy at success, the same heart-burnings at failure, as have always accompanied such efforts. The difference between what obtained then and what holds good now, is that money alone was useless as a weapon for beating down the barriers, whereas now it is, if not the chief, at least one of the most potent of means to that end. But it is only in this respect that a comparison between the two periods can be instituted; for in everything else things have changed so completely; life has taken on so complicated a form; the classes have, through so many indirect causes, become so mixed; that when we read of certain doings and sayings emanating from the earlier time, we seem to be transported into a state of society which has practically no resemblance to that of our own day. Although this is so, we must remember that such records as have come down to us are nearly wholly concerned with the one small body of men and women who formed the high society of the day, and that the life of a large number of London's inhabitants bore a not so dissimilar likeness to what obtains now.

The merchant class had risen to great affluence. The Napoleonic struggle which was death to so many was to a large number a source of wealth and influence. Fortunes were made rapidly, and often lost as quickly; and if I again mention the names of the Sedleys and Osbornes it is because these point, through the medium of their creator's genius, a moral bearing on this subject, and exhibit representative examples of how commerce could smile and frown on its votaries. Just as the best pictures of this class, that lived in the substantial houses of Bloomsbury and possessed their villas at Clapham and Edmonton, Richmond and Roehampton, Highgate and Tottenham, have been left us by one of the outstanding novelists of the day, so have the personages of the Law and Finance been drawn by another, and in Mr. Tulkinghorn " of the Fields," we get the type of the old-fashioned lawyer (perhaps a little exaggerated, but a no less telling portrait for that) who lived in his offices but was at home in a score of great houses whose secrets he knew so intimately; and Mr. Merdle, the example of the financier whose splendid establishment in Harley Street and whose sphinx-like attitude towards his fellows, concealed from the world the monetary ramifications that finally led to disgrace and suicide—circumstances which are said to have been based on the actual case of Sadleir, the fraudulent banker.

The physicians congregated in Great Ormond Street; and Gower Street teemed with barristers in good practise, although a house in Russell Square was looked upon as the highest aim of a specially successful and ambitious legal man. Those wealthy nabobs who had returned from the service of the East India Company or from other remunerative posts, migrated, as if by instinct, to Portland Place and Harley Street, until a later period when they built splendid houses for themselves in Kensington Palace Gardens or took large mansions in other West-end resorts.

Many of the better classes used handsome equipages, types of which are shown on Plate 64; some drove four-in-hands (the Four in Hand Club had been founded in 1808 (Plate 66); and among the wealthy, coachmen wore the three cornered hats and bob-wigs, and footmen, hanging on behind the carriages, the silk stockings, which in later days seldom made their appearance except at Drawing Rooms and such-like royal and official functions (Plate 28). When travelling into the country, outriders were not infrequently seen preceding the carriages of the great. In fact, the decorative note which had been such a marked accompaniment to the 18th century, still lingered on, in spite of the general change in style of life and manners of dress; and it formed, for many a year after the beginning of the 19th century, a rather painful contrast with the condition of the larger section of the population of London. For there is no doubt that cheek by jowl with these outward evidences of wealth and well-being, the capital comprised a vast number of people whose destitution was terrible, and a large number whose means of existence was painfully precarious.

Industry did not dream of the organization which in our day has perhaps gone to the other extreme. Nowadays women do every-

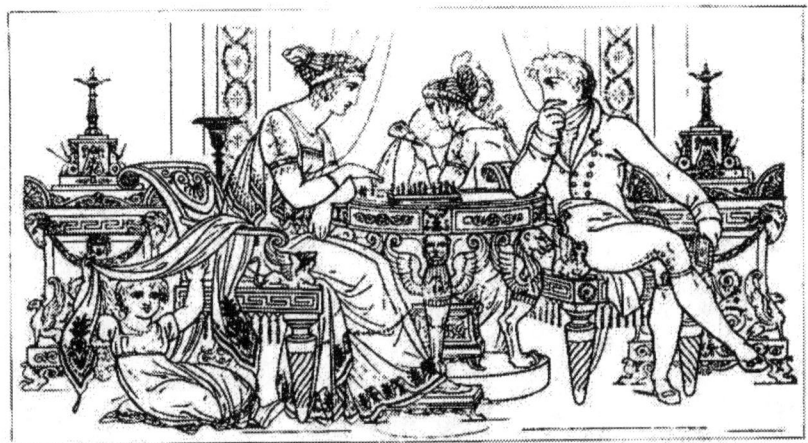
A Game of Chess

A Game of Cards

Drinking Tea

INDOOR OCCUPATIONS (1823)

By H. Moses

A Meet of the Hounds at Matching Green

An Archery Meeting

Partridge-shooting

COUNTRY AMUSEMENTS

From Contemporary Prints

thing; then they were debarred from all sorts of occupations which would seem to be specially within their province ; and we are told that it was " no uncommon thing to see men employed in the most effeminate branches of art and commerce," the man-milliner being one of the most conspicuous classes of these innovators, a class which a contemporary writer disdainfully alludes to as " perfumed coxcombs measuring the riband or folding the gauze."

If the lot of the lower strata of society and of the employés generally was bad, that of the master tradesman was, taken as a whole, excellent. There was little competition in the earlier days of the period; indeed, there does not seem to have been a sufficiency of shops to supply adequately the needs of the Metropolis ; the consequence being that the shop-keepers had plenty of custom (Plates 38 & 39), and were under no necessity of expending the vast sums in advertisement which they are often, to-day, obliged to do. With the progress of time great changes took place in this respect, and when the half-century was reached there is abundance of evidence in the newspapers alone to show that competition had become more pronounced and the advertising medium a necessity.

The same gradual development took place in another aspect of commercial life. During the earlier years the status of education, even among quite important tradesmen, was painfully low ; and this was due to what we should now regard as an almost incredible reason : a prejudice on the part of a customer to deal with anyone if it were known that he cared for literature ! So astounding a proposition would not be believed were it not proved by the evidence of Francis Place, a military tailor in Pall Mall, who, giving evidence in 1835 before a Select Committee of the House of Commons, on the subject of Education, stated that in the year 1812, he had lost a good customer because that gentleman accidentally discovered that he possessed and read works of an historical and metaphysical character !

The amusements of this class were restricted in an extraordinary degree ; and in the evening, unless the cheaper places at the play— and there were only a relatively few opportunities for this— appealed to him he was obliged to resort to the tap-room of some neighbouring public-house where lotteries and punch clubs—" Free and Easys " and " Cock and Hen Clubs," as they were called, often resulted in his moral and financial ruin. The more sedate stayed at home; but the younger ones, especially the apprentices (apprenticeship was the general rule in most handicrafts then) who required some outlet for their energies, not infrequently roamed about the streets and made night hideous by noise and generally disorderly conduct, and if aquainted with the scientific use of their fists, as very many were, were ready to resent by blows any interference with their gambols. Nothing shows so markedly the necessity for Peel's system of police regulation as the conduct of these irresponsible young hot-heads who could point to the example of many a youthful blood of birth as an excuse for breaking windows, wrenching off knockers, or disturbing the slumbers of the Charlies whose business it was supposed to be to keep order in the streets.

"Fashions and Frights of 1829," by George Cruikshank

SETTLING DAY AT TATTERSALL'S (1836)

By James Pollard

FASHIONS FOR 1839

CHAPTER III.

SOCIAL CENTRES.

THE two outstanding social centres in London during the earlier years of the 19th century were Holland House and Gore House (Plate 34), and it is these that most frequently recur in the memoirs and letters of the period. Both of them have, indeed, taken on something of a classic air; they form part, not only of the social, but also of the political and literary, history of the times, and it is probable that no two mansions in the Metropolis are better known by name, or have a wider European celebrity, than these two, so dissimilar in architecture, so different in their ultimate fates; but in both of which all the finest intellects of the day at one time or another foregathered.

Holland House happily remains; its fabric not only sentient with the outstanding personalities which thronged its chambers during the later years of George III's reign until the earlier ones of Queen Victoria's; but its architectural features preserved from that great period which saw the building of Hatfield and the completion of Longleat. It is London's one and only example of the domestic architecture of that far away time, and has been so since 1878, when Northumberland House (Plate 15), went the way of all bricks and mortar. Macaulay, so frequent a visitor, once foresaw the day when this glorious pile would give place to the rows of terraces which seemed then to be throwing their length all over the West-end Mercifully his prophesy is not yet fulfilled, and Holland House embowered among the trees that whisper of Addison and dream of Fox, is still one of London's most valuable architectural assets.

Gore House no longer exists. It stood at the west end of Prince's Gate, and those who listen to the concord of sweet sounds in the Albert Hall or dance in its arena, are doing so practically on the spot where Lady Blessington and Count D'Orsay received that crowd of illustrious ones whose names have power to thrill us even in these prosaic days. If Holland House is associated with great names before the period of its social eminence arrived—those of Addison and Fairfax, Lambert and Fox—Gore House can boast the one time residence within it of William Wilberforce, who lived here from 1808 to 1821, and who, if Sidney Smith's dictum that " the noblest occupation of a man was to make other men free and happy," be correct, may be regarded as a greater man than those whose presence further dignified the dignity of Holland House.

But although these two great centres of social life are the outstanding examples, they were not the only ones, and before saying anything further about them it will be convenient to notice two or three others.

Royal palaces are proverbially the rallying points of Society, and as such Carlton House during the first half of the century and Buckingham Palace during the second, should be mentioned. From 1783 to 1825 George IV, as Prince of Wales, Regent and King, lived in Carlton House (Plates 31 & 32), which Holland had reconstructed out of the earlier residence of the Princess Dowager of Wales (George III's mother). In the latter year, however, he went to Buckingham House which had been altered and enlarged, and had become Buckingham Palace (Plates 29 & 34). William IV, however, never lived there, regarding the place as unsightly and uncomfortable;[1] but on the accession of Queen Victoria it was again altered, by Blore, and the Sovereign took up her residence there in July, 1837. It was not, however, till 1850 that the same architect added the east façade and removed the Marble Arch, which had been standing in front of the palace for many years, to approximately its present site.

Under George IV, Carlton House was the centre of that coterie which numbered Brummell and Colonel Hanger, and the band of satellites radiating round the royal luminary. Here Tom Moore sang his own lyrics, and Theodore Hook exercised his marvellous powers as an "improvisatore"; here Wellington listened grimly to the Prince Regent's statement that he led the Guards at Waterloo, and on being referred to for corroboration replied, " I have often heard you say so, Sir "; here took place the memorable dinner at which the Prince tried to unmask the author of " Waverley," when Scott parried the toast proposed, by exclaiming " I will let the real Simon Pure know of the honour that has been done him "; to which the Prince rejoined, "Here's to the health of Walter Scott—got you there Walter, my boy ! "; here the Princess Charlotte was married, at nine o'clock at night, on May 2nd 1816, in the great

[1] The Duke of Wellington, addressing the House of Lords, in July, 1828, said that, notwithstanding all that had been done, " No sovereign in Europe' perhaps no private gentleman, is as ill lodged as the King of this country." And Creevy calls it " The Devil's Own."

SOCIAL CENTRES

Crimson Room—an apartment described with such particularity in Pierce Egan's[1] "Life in London."

On special occasions great fêtes and gala dinners were given at Carlton House, and, particularly, in 1814, the visit of the allied sovereigns made it a scene of regal festivity. But except on such occasions it was hardly a place where ladies found themselves with any ease or credit, and it may therefore be dismissed as not so much a social centre, as the home of a sybarite who in defiance of public opinion surrounded himself by those of both sexes who were bound to obey the royal mandate or who gladly went there to bask in its hot (both actual and metaphorical) atmosphere.

As time elapses it becomes increasingly difficult to estimate accurately the character of the Royal host of Carlton House. The charm of Thackeray's style has clothed his denunciations with an air of almost apostolic force; Mr. Max Beerbohm's beauty of diction has, on the other hand, been thrown into the scale of the defence and forms a sort of palliative to the fierce onslaughts of the older man. What seems to emerge is a figure, rather legendary to us now, of one who, without wise guidance, threw himself into that life of pleasure which unfolded itself to him, and drank from its cups to the dregs, rather as a resource from tedium than from any specially inherent bad qualities. Such a man as George III, narrow and bigoted, with the ideas of a despotic farmer, whose home life was the quintessence of the dull and commonplace, was just the one to produce a re-action of a violent kind in his children. Distrusted, thwarted, treated with suspicion, George the younger, whose natural gifts were far above the average, who was clever and not ill-educated, became spoiled by those whose interest it was to create antagonism to a higher authority; and from being the tool gradually became the head and front of an opposition to the royal authority. But he did not reach this stage until he had tried all sorts of devices to create a better understanding with his father. It is often supposed that it was entirely the Prince's fault that that estrangement (to which Queen Charlotte was also a party) was brought about, and from these false premises a wrong conclusion has been reached. It was rather due to that curse which made a breach between George I and his son and George II and his, and which seemed to have descended to another generation of the Guelph family.

[1] Probably the most complete description of the interior of Carlton House is that given in this curious book, wherein we are told how Tom, Jerry, Bob Logic, Kate and Sue, visit the gorgeous abode of their ruler.

LIFE IN REGENCY AND EARLY VICTORIAN TIMES

Treated differently, George, Prince of Wales (Plate 17), might reasonably have been credited with turning out a very different man. He possessed a generous nature, he was easy and affable, he was clement and forgiving, he was indeed a Prince Charming who through adverse circumstances became a byword. His treatment of his wife cannot be defended, but at least two pleas in extenuation may be entered on his behalf: He was forced into the marriage against his will, although his debts which made it necessary were of his own creation; and the lady was impossible in every way—in looks, in manners, in a vulgarity which must have been torture to him, but was just of that free and easy character (as being exemplified in a royal personage) which appealed to the mob and made it her constant ally.

Another great house of social entertainment in which, however, in spite of a fashionable veneer, politics was the moving spirit, was *Devonshire House*, where the 5th Duke and his beautiful Duchess, Georgina (who died in 1806—five years before her husband) extended that gorgeous hospitality whose annals are so interlinked with those of the Whig party and the career of its great protagonist, Charles James Fox. Under the 6th Duke, who was unmarried, the reputation of Devonshire House for social entertaining was fully kept up; and the fine looking host (Leslie says he was over six feet in height, and Macaulay records his princely air and manner) received here a crowd of notable people, till his death in 1858; seven years before which event he had turned his mansion into a theatre for the Guild of Literature and Art to perform Lytton's " Not so bad as we seem," with Dickens and other splendid strollers as the actors.

Lansdowne House was another political, social, and scientific centre where Priestley had been sheltered, and where the third Marquis of Lansdowne, the Nestor of the Liberal Party, who, in the words of the Princess Lieven, was " the most distinguished of the great aristocrats of this country, without a spot on his great reputation,"formed the present fine collection of pictures, and was a generous and splendid patron of art and literature. His sympathies were with the modern as well as with the ancient schools in both arts, and Leslie painted for him many of those *genre* pictures which are so essentially of their period but which recall the manners and customs of an earlier day.

Yet another outstanding meeting place for social and literary celebrities was the famous little house in *St. James's Place* where

SOCIAL CENTRES

Rogers uttered his caustic remarks, but so often also showed his generosity, and in which every object was, as Byron once remarked, sentient of the cultivated mind of the banker-poet. It is impossible, within prescribed limits, to give even the barest record of those who were entertained in this house, either at its host's well-known breakfasts or at other times. Peruse a list of the great ones in literature, science, art, or society, and there will hardly be found one who was not at one time or another to be encountered here. But, as in the case of Lord Lansdowne and the Duke of Devonshire, there was no *chatelaine* at 22, St. James's Place,[1] and, in consequence, the society which gathered in the three hospitable houses just mentioned was largely, although not exclusively, restricted to the sterner sex. In the case of Holland House and Gore House it was otherwise, and although neither Lady Holland nor Lady Blessington was regarded by many social leaders as quite conforming to the rigid ethics required by the super-exclusiveness of certain coteries, yet they *were* hostesses and made their power felt among the great ladies of the period in no uncertain way. If they never achieved the extraordinary influence which radiated from the Lady Patronesses of Almack's, or preserved in their salons the select quality that attached to the réunions in King Street, their receptions were not the less amusing and desirable for that, and many a votary of fashion, male or female, must have sighed, amidst the paradise of the High Temple of Fashion, for the picturesque rooms where they were likely to be snubbed by the incorrigible Lady Holland, or the more factitious salon where Lady Blessington received them with her charming welcome, and the gorgeous Count, "the Phœbus-Apollo of Dandyism" as Carlyle called him, with his consummate tact and good breeding.

The annals of Holland House have been written by Princess Liechtenstein, and there is literally hardly a volume of memoirs or letters dealing with this period, in which allusions are not to be found to the place and its owners. It has become historic. There the outspoken opinions of Lady Holland, the gentle acceptance of such by Lord Holland, the witticisms of Luttrell, the didactic periods of Macaulay, Allen's scholarship and Hook's

---

[1] It is not generally remembered that Miss Rogers, sister of the poet, lived in Regent's Park and gave breakfasts," a sort of imitation, and not a bad one either, of her brother's in St. James's" says Ticknor who records visiting there in June, 1838. According to the same authority the lady was almost as great a collector of pictures and bric-à-brac as her famous brother.

improvisations, all had play. Some of the descriptions of these symposia are famous, Macaulay's, for instance,[1] and the diaries of strangers, like Ticknor, prove the cosmopolitanism that reigned here. Everyone who was anyone was welcome, and the cordial reception of the host more than counterbalanced the rather awe-inspiring directness of the famous Lady Holland. Sometimes the réunions were select in number, at others the crowd must have been anything but agreeable, and there is the story of Lady Holland, on the entrance of another guest to the table, calling out to Luttrell, " Make room, Mr. Luttrell," to receive the witty reply : " It will, indeed, be to make it, Lady Holland, for it does not exist."

This phase [2] of the social greatness of Holland House lasted from 1799 to 1840, in the October of which latter year Lord Holland died ; so that as a rallying point for all that was best and greatest in politics, science, art and literature, it practically covered the period dealt with in this book. Although it is probable that many illustrious ones went there for the gratification to be obtained from Lord Holland's delightful society, there is no doubt that his lady was the ruling spirit, and not a few of the guests must have snatched a fearful joy in submitting themselves to her snubs and sarcasm—she who could never break Sheridan of using the word " gentlemanly," could tell Macaulay to " ring the bell," or Lord John Russell to " lay down that screen ; you will spoil it," or Allen to " take a candle and show Mr. Cradock the picture of Buonaparte." Well might the great historian of the day say that " The centurion did not keep his soldiers in better order than she keeps her guests. It is to one ' Go,' and he goeth ; and to another ' Do this,' and it is done."

The society at Gore House was still more eclectic than was that at Holland House. Lady Blessington (Plate 25) had lived much abroad and she had pretensions to be considered a writer. Both circumstances helped to make her sympathies with bohemianism more pronounced than was the case with her rival *chatelaine*, and therefore, although her rooms saw the presence of many of the leaders of Society, there were also to be found in them many

[1] See, for example, his amusing account, in a letter to his sister dated May 30th, 1831.

[2] I say advisedly " this phase," because another followed when those famous garden parties which some of us still remember as outstanding social functions of the season during our youth, took place under a later and more charming hostess.

SOCIAL CENTRES

whose names enjoyed but a restricted celebrity, and some whose claim to notice at all arose rather from notoriety.

Without entering into the details of her biography, it may be stated that although Gore House saw the apothoesis of her social success, it was not the only house in London in which Lady Blessington surrounded herself with notabilities. Before her marriage to Lord Blessington she had, as Miss Power, lived, in 1816 and again in 1818, in Manchester Square. After her marriage she went to 10, St. James's Square, which her husband had taken and beautified for her reception. Here they remained till Lord Blessington's death; after which event, having but an income of £2,000 a year, she gave the place up as being too expensive, and went to live in Seamore Place,[1] where she inaugurated that "salon" with which her name is identified. But it was at Gore House, which she took in the early part of 1836, that her receptions reached the *apogee* of their splendour and renown. At the same time there is no doubt that during the whole period Lady Blessington was living here, she laboured under constant anxiety due to monetary troubles. Her expenditure is said to have been just double the jointure she received, and although she must have made considerable sums by her pen, these were not sufficient to meet the expenses of continual entertaining, added to D'Orsay's extravagance of living. She is credited with having regulated her household with infinite care, but relative economy is useless if general expenditure is beyond income. The crash came in 1849, and on April 14th of that year Lady Blessington and the two Miss Powers, who lived with her, joined Count D'Orsay in Paris whither he had fled a fortnight earlier.

In the following month the contents of the mansion were sold by auction, and Madden gives an account of the sale and the crowds that attended it. Lady Blessington's French manservant also wrote details to his mistress, and speaking of those old habitués who came to the last scene, he makes the well-known remark that "c'est peut être M. Thackeray, qui est la seule personne que j'ai vu réellement affecté en votre départ." There must have been many others who were, however, although they may not have

---

[1] Madden says "Perhaps the *agrémèns* of Seamore Place surpassed those of the Gore House *soirées*." Willis in his "Pencillings by the Way," gives a long description of a visit paid by him to Seamore Place, which Madden, whose three volumes are an *alla podrida* of interesting facts badly presented, gives in full. See "Life and Correspondence of Lady Blessington," 3 vols., 1855.

shewn it; for it is quite clear from the innumerable references to the hostess and to D'Orsay, in the pages of contemporary letter-writers, so many of whom were constant guests, that both of these spoiled children of fashion were capable of inspiring regard and even affection.

When the drawing-rooms of Gore House were lighted up and filled with the heterogeneous throng that was accustomed to assemble there, the effect must have been as brilliant as the conversation. Lady Blessington seated on her well-known *fauteuil* might have been seen listening to the witticisms of Luttrell, Theodore Hook, or Sidney Smith; or with mock solemnity attending to M. Julien le Jeune, while, at the instances of D'Orsay, he recited one of his lengthy and lugubrious "Chagrins Politiques." There Dickens vied with Thackeray, and Ainsworth with Lytton, in the glory of embroidered waistcoats and the height of snowy billowing cravats; and there L. E. L. appeared "the very personification of Brompton."[1] Trelawny there repeated his memories of Byron and Shelley, and Lord Chesterfield gave forth his gastronomic reminiscences. Hither Bernal Osborne and Monckton Milnes brought witty word pictures from the House, and Sheridan Knowles and Albany Fonblanque news from the theatre from which Liston and Macready would occasionally tear themselves. Liszt and Rubini represented music, and Lawrence art; while Lord Wellesley would sometimes come in from neighbouring Kingston House, and his more famous brother from Hyde Park Corner. The classic Landor and the dithyrambic Moore and Disraeli of the raven locks, with his imperturbable air, would help to give an added distinction to rooms whose note, borrowed from the hostess and the great Dandy of the day, was itself one of supreme distinction.

What Gore House looked like externally at this period may be seen from the accompanying illustration (Plate 34). This then outlying part of London has become changed out of all knowledge, but one mansion still remains, Kingston House, to recall the day when a few large residences existed here, in place of the rows of houses and the amazing rotunda that now occupy the sites of them and their ample gardens; before that hideous germanized eyesore—the Albert Memorial—was unhappily thought of.

As we have seen, Holland House existed as a great social centre during the first forty years of the 19th century; Gore House, on the

[1] Disraeli in a letter to his sister.

COUNT D'ORSAY
From a Contemporary Engraving

THE COUNTESS OF BLESSINGTON
From a Painting by E. T. Parris

"5 O'clock in Hyde Park." (The Central Figure on Horseback is a Portrait of Sir Lumley Skeffington)

By "C. H."

other hand, for little more than the last decade of that period ; while other great houses enjoyed a longer or shorter term of social fame, although not one has left its impress on the life of the time so markedly as have these two.

Anyone aquainted with contemporary fashionable annals will not need to be reminded that there were many other hostesses whose names were famous ; whose réunions were crowded ; whose mansions were centres of political or artistic coteries, or a combination of both. There was, for instance, Lady Charleville, whose receptions at *Charleville House*, Cavendish Square, came near to rivalling those at Gore House—so agreeable was the society, so intellectual the conversation, to be found there. Lady Charleville died in 1851, and for many years preceding this event she had lost the use of her legs and might have been seen being carried to the carriage or bath-chair which she constantly used.[1]

Then there was Lady Morgan, "the wild Irish girl," who lived at *No. 11, William Street*, opposite Albert Gate, whose Sunday afternoons and evenings were thronged gatherings, in a smaller way, till her death in 1859; but above all, there was that redoubtable old Lady Cork, who has become something of a legendary figure, and who as Miss Monckton had been one of Dr. Johnson's favourites. This wonderful old lady died at her house in *New Burlington Street*, on May 20th, 1840, aged ninety-four. Rivalling Ninon de L'Enclos in her gift of perpetual youth, Lady Cork (she married Lord Cork in 1784) enjoyed society and the theatre almost till the last, and New Burlington Street became the centre of a remarkable assemblage of wits, politicians, artists, and authors linked up with the fine flower of the *haute noblesse*. Her Sunday parties were the first that were unaccompanied by gambling which had hitherto been a regular part of such gatherings. It has been said of her that " her social reputation dates from her attempts, the first of the kind in England, to introduce into the routine and formation of our high life, something of the wit and energy which characterized the society of Paris in the last (18th) century. While still young, she made the house of her mother, Lady Galway, the point of rendezvous, where talent and genius might mingle with rank and fashion, and the advantages of intellectual endowments be mutually exchanged."

In the pages of Charles Greville, and even more so in those of his

---

[1] See Abraham Hayward's Correspondence, for many references to this gifted lady.

brother Henry, who was not so interested in politics as was his elder, will be found many references to less famous salons which have now become forgotten (an outstanding one during the latter part of the period was that of Lady Palmerston in Piccadilly), but which during their day exercised an influence on the life of the upper classes, and added to their possibilities of amusement. Although Mrs. Montagu died in 1801, and the learned Mrs. Carter in 1806, neither of these blue-stockings belonged to the London of the new century. They were but survivors of an earlier period whose manners and customs were passing away, and the Portman Square of the one and the Clarges Street of the other were entering on a new phase of London's history. Miss Berry survived later into the century, and was to know Scott and be on terms of intimacy with Rogers; but she, too, preserved in Half Moon Street a flavour of a day that was gone; and the Piccadilly, whence the famous light over her front door could be seen, was no longer the Piccadilly of " Old Q," but the strolling ground of the Brummells and Alvanleys and Seftons who made the period decorative until D'Orsay made it dignified.

In the immediate vicinity of London there were a number of large houses—villas they used to be called—many of which were social centres, especially during the summer months when fêtes and garden parties were held in their grounds. Of these the most important was the far-famed *Chiswick House* (Plate 36), where Fox and Canning both died, and where splendid entertainments, such as those given to the Allied Sovereigns in 1814, to Queen Victoria in 1842, and to the Emperor of Russia in 1844, formed social landmarks, continued down to our own day. There was also *Gunnersbury House*, then as now belonging to the Rothschild family, and *Kenwood*, that beautiful example of the Adams' work, at that time the property of the Earl of Mansfield, the son of its original builder; *Hurlingham House*, where the club is now; *Lonsdale House*, Fulham, the seat then of Sir John Shelley; *Brandenburg House*, where Bubb Dodington once lived and the Margravine of Anspach, and where, in the earlier years of the 19th century, Queen Caroline kept her court and was congratulated on the result of her trial by thousands of well-wishers.

Besides these places and innumerable others of less importance,[1] there were the more distant mansions where society went to enjoy

[1] See for notice of many of them, " The Beauties of Middlesex," by William Keane, 1850.

PLATE 27

A Fashionable Gaming-house (1823) *By W. Heath*

A Fashionable Coffee-house (1825) *By Theodore Lane*

A Card-party at Home (1820) *By T. Rowlandson*

MIDDAY TRAFFIC IN PARLIAMENT STREET (1829)

By E. Lami & H. Monnier

PLATE 28

SOCIAL CENTRES

rural pleasures in the midst of the London season, such as Sion House, Osterley Park, and Strawberry Hill, all of which are associated with those garden parties and *fêtes champêtres* which have always appealed to the Londoner jaded by the heat and bustle of the Metropolis.

I speak of another social centre—Almack's—last because, although it carries us far from such rustic delights, it is too important to be dismissed in a few sentences.

ALMACK'S

This famous place of entertainment (Plates 11a & 38), which is more closely associated with the society of the later eighteenth and earlier nineteenth centuries than any other institution, was founded by William Macall, or Almack as he spelt his name, in 1764. The year before he had started the club of the same name in Pall Mall, which was afterwards removed to St. James's Street and became, later, Brooks's. The idea of such a place no doubt occurred to Almack in consequence of the success of Mrs. Cornelys's well-known venture at Carlisle House, Soho Square, where, however, the licence permitted had alienated many of the supporters of " the Heidegger of the age."

Almack saw that another form of attraction was necessary, and found it, not in a mixed but in a select company. He chose his site well, in the centre of club-land and in touch with St. James's and Pall Mall. He obtained leases of various properties immediately to the east of Pall Mall Place, and commissioned Robert Mylne to design a suite of assembly rooms on their sites. In 1764 the building was begun, and in the February of the following year formally opened, although, notwithstanding the presence of a royal duke, not under particularly promising conditions.

At a later period Almack's became merely an assembly for dancing, but it was also at this period a kind of ladies' club; and while cotillons were taking place in the great room, money was being gambled away in other parts of the building, with an energy that might even have surprised Crockfords and a regularity that was hardly surpassed at White's.

From early records one gets many a foretaste of the later despotism of Almack's, which rejected and blackballed with a freedom that made its name a byword in the society of the day. During the first phase of Almack's it was of a rather heterogeneous character; there was dancing, but there was also much more;

gambling and gossip and a female club-life not very dissimilar from the men's fraternities that surrounded it in Pall Mall and St. James's Street. In its second phase it became a centre for dancing and nothing else. Its character for *selectness*, however, was not merely retained but amplified; the laws of the Medes and Persians found themselves figuring in a ninteenth century revival, and it is safe to say that no personal authority, no special endowments, no mere wealth or influence, outside the magic circle, could avail if those who possessed such attributes attempted to break through its ironbound rules. The memoirs and letters of the period are full of references to the rooms in King Street and to those who ruled over their destinies. Of all these authorities Captain Gronow is the most circumstantial and, inasmuch as he was both in and of the world about which he writes, the most reliable. Let us see what he has to say about Almack's in the year of grace 1814.

"At the present time," he writes, "one can hardly conceive the importance which was attached to getting admission to Almack's, the seventh heaven of the fashionable world." Only half-a-dozen out of some three hundred officers of the Guards " were honoured with vouchers of admission to this exclusive temple . . . . Many diplomatic arts, much finesse and a host of intrigues, were set in motion to get an invitation." The slightest infraction of the Lady Patronesses'—(that female oligarchy, less in numbers but equal in power to the "Venetian Council of Ten" as Grantley Berkeley remarks)—Draconic laws, was visited with sternest reprisals. Even the Duke of Wellington was once turned from the portals of Almack's, because he was wearing trousers and not the knee-breeches which had been made indispensable by the Committee sitting in solemn conclave. No wonder Lady Clementine Davies remarks that "at Almack's in 1814 the rules were very strict"; while a writer in the New Monthly Magazine adds " this is selection with a vengeance; the very quintessence of aristocracy. Three fourths of the nobility knock in vain for admission. Into this *sanctum sanctorum*, of course, the sons of commerce never think of entering." However, there must have been some laxity later, for we are told that " into this very blue chamber, in the absence of the six necromancers (the lady patronesses) have the votaries of trade contrived to intrude themselves."

But not as yet was such a desecration to take place. Gronow proceeds: " Very often persons whose rank and fortunes entitled

The Company Going to and Returning from the King's Drawing-Room at Old Buckingham Palace; with a View of the Green Park and Piccadilly in the Distance (1822)

From a Contemporary Print

PLATE 29

BROOKS' CLUB: THE INTERIOR OF THE GREAT
SUBSCRIPTION ROOM (1825)
By Robert Cruikshank

A GAMING-ROOM AT CROCKFORD'S (1825)
By Robert Cruikshank

PLATE 31

VIEW OF ST. JAMES' STREET, AT THE COMMENCEMENT
OF THE XIXTH CENTURY   *Drawn by T. Malton*

THE ENTRANCE FRONT TO CARLTON HOUSE
Drawn by C. Wild (1817)   *Henry Holland, Architect*

A CORNER OF THE GOLDEN DRAWING-ROOM
Drawn by C. Wild (1817)

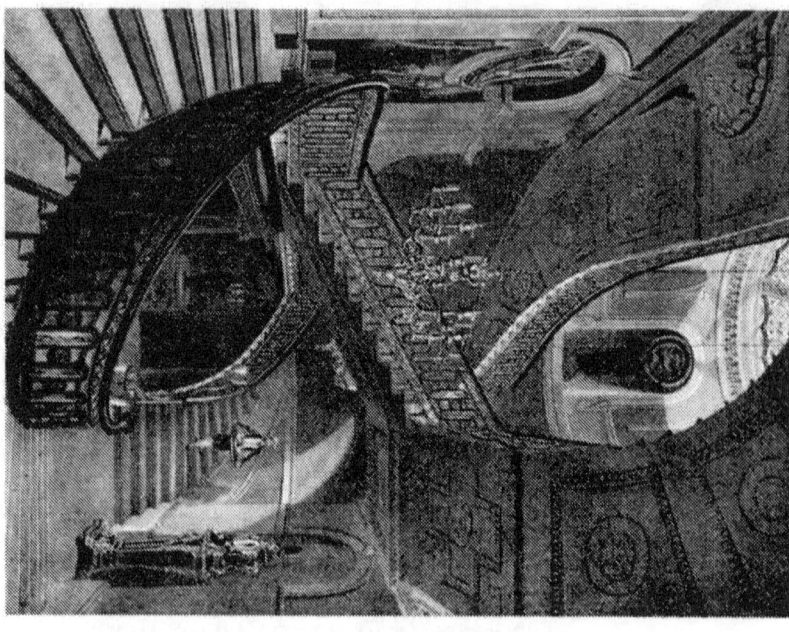

THE GREAT STAIRCASE
Henry Holland, Architect

EXAMPLES OF THE "DIRECTOIRE" MODE AT CARLTON HOUSE

SOCIAL CENTRES

them to the *entrée* anywhere, were excluded by the cliqueism of the lady patronesses, for the female government of Almack's was a pure despotism, and subject to all the caprices of despotic rule: it is needless to add that, like every other despotism, it was not innocent of abuse." Those who, in 1814, arrogated to themselves a more than royal sway, were Lady Castlereagh, Princess Esterhazy, Lady Cowper, Lady Jersey, Mrs Drummond Burrell, afterwards Lady Willoughby D'Eresby, Lady Sefton, and the Princess Lieven. Of these Lady Cowper was the most popular, Lady Jersey, according to Gronow, sometimes made herself "simply ridiculous" with her tragedy-queen airs, and was not infrequently ill-bred in her manners; Lady Sefton was kind and Princess Lieven haughty, and Lady Castlereagh and Mrs. Burrell were both too *grandes dames* to be anything but picturesque and exclusive figure heads.

The dances were at first extremely insular in character, being confined to Scotch reels, and what Gronow terms "the old English country dance," which, however, was really a rendering of the French *contre danse*, and had nothing particularly bucolic about it. Neil Gow, the Scotch violinist, directed the orchestra on these occasions. In 1815, however, a change came over the terpsichorean fare provided. In that year Lady Jersey, returning from Paris, brought with her the quadrille. Gronow, in an access of enthusiasm for the dance which, as he rightly says, has so long remained popular, gives the names of those who took part in the first quadrille ever danced in England. Lady Jersey was one and she was supported by Lady Susan Ryder, Miss Montgomery and Lady Harriett Butler; while the men were the Count St. Aldegonde, Mr. Montagu, Mr. Montgomery[1] and Mr. Charles Standish[2].

On the heels of the quadrille came the waltz, which created a tremendous sensation, and there were not many who at first ventured to whirl round Almack's rooms in the dance which Byron has described so vividly. After a time, however, its strangeness passed off, and "that laughing philosopher gallant and gay," Lord Palmerston, might have been seen dancing it with the haughty Princess Lieven in his arms. Indeed, the waltzing mania seems to

---

[1] He was one of the Stewards of Almack's and a member of the coterie of Dandies.

[2] In Gronow's "Reminiscences" there is an illustration showing Lord and Lady Worcester, Lady Jersey and Clanronald Macdonald "dancing the first quadrille." I don't know how the author reconciled his statement in the text with that on this picture.

have turned the heads of Society which thus disported itself "with unparalleled assiduity," not only at Almack's, but elsewhere. The introduction of this form of the dance is by some said to have been due to Princess Lieven, who brought it from the Continent in 1816, but Raikes affirms that it came to this country three years earlier, and Gronow places its importation in 1815. Some of its most finished exponents were, naturally enough, foreigners resident in England, and Baron de Neumann and Baron Tripp rivalled St. Aldegonde and M. Bourblanc in their gyrations. Prince Leopold of Sax Coburg and Count D'Orsay were also exponents of merit, and the Dukes of Beaufort and Devonshire, Lords Londonderry and Anglesea and Dongall, all showed themselves singularly adept in it.

One of the rules of Almack's was that no one was permitted to enter after eleven o'clock at night; and Ticknor[1] tells us how, on one occasion, the Duke of Wellington (who seems to have been unfortunate in his relations with the place) arriving at seven minutes past that hour, was peremptorily turned away by order of Lady Jersey. On another occasion the Duke was behind time again, but was then admitted, the rule being waived in his favour, at the earnest solicitation of one of the Patronesses. Although it was well-nigh impossible to break through the rules and to escape the notice of the lynx-eyed janitors, a certain peer once succeeded in doing both. It was in this wise: Owing to an accident to his carriage the nobleman in question arrived after 11 o'clock. Instead of attempting to gain admittance which he knew would be useless, he waited outside until some of his friends came out. He then went up to their carriage and pretended to see them into it, as another gentleman, a friend of his, who had left the rooms for that purpose, was also doing. As the carriage drove off, the noble lord followed his friend in again; the latter truthfully telling the servants at the door that they had merely been seeing some ladies into their carriage.

Moore's Diary contains many references to Almack's. Moore had the *entrée*, and made good use of the privilege, and on one occasion he tells with satisfaction how Lady Jersey and Lady Tankerville " were sending various messengers after me through the room," on which he was subsequently bantered by the Duchess of Sussex at a ball at Devonshire House. In 1822 he is found remarking that the place was " not quite what it used to be."

[1]Diary vol. 1, p.245.

SOCIAL CENTRES

Perhaps the poet was out of humour; for Almack's vogue had not yet begun to wane by any means. Indeed, we find Ticknor, in 1835, remarking on the brilliance of the assembly; and what he noticed chiefly was the greater youth of the company than was formerly the case. Some modification of the rules had, however, evidently taken place, for, not only does he observe that there was no ceremony, no regulation, no managing, but that he and his party arrived "just before the doors were closed at *mid-night*." A foot-note in Luttrell's "Advice to Julia," where Almack's bulks largely, as readers of that amusing skit are aware, says: "It was till very lately settled that even *after* half past eleven the whole string of coaches then formed in the street might deposit its contents in the ball room. By this equitable construction, many were admitted after mid-night, but now (circa 1827) the hour of limitation has been enlarged till twelve o'clock and the privilege of the string abolished."

By 1840 there really does seem to have been some signs of decadence at Almack's, and a writer in the Quarterly Review for that year remarks on it and draws the inference that it is "a clear proof that the palmy days of exclusiveness are gone by in England," and he adds "although it is obviously impossible to prevent any given number of persons from congregating and re-establishing an oligarchy, we are quite sure that the attempt would be ineffectual, and that *the sense of their importance would extend little beyond the set.*" In these words, which I have italicized, is adumbrated the remarkable power of Almack's in its prime. Its influence and importance extended far beyond the set that composed it. At no time did more than 200 persons congregate within its walls; its patronesses numbered less than a dozen; but its fame was a by-word throughout the land; its power unquestioned and unassailable. To be introduced into the magic circle was, at one time, regarded as a greater distinction than being presented at Court, and was more difficult of attainment. The names of Lady Jersey, Lady Londonderry, Lady Cowper, Lady Sefton, Princess Lieven, Princess Esterhazy, and Mrs. Burrell are of continual recurrence in the pages of contemporary memoirs; Sir William Fraser, in his gossiping ana, has recorded anecdotes of them. Lord Lamington[1] has left his quota of criticism and admiration. When one reads stories of the despotic manners of these great ladies, one is inclined to think of them as haughty and unapproachable; but this was not always

[1] 'In the days of the Dandies'.

LIFE IN REGENCY AND EARLY VICTORIAN TIMES

the case. What they all combined in effecting was the segregation of a certain class—and the very quintessence of that class—from the attempts of interlopers armed with nothing but impertinence and money.

If here and there people, not of the first rank, procured an entrance to Almack's, it will be found to have been accorded for some special gift (not of money) with which they were endowed: Brummell, of course, was given it, because of the position he had made for himself in Society; Moore, because of his social qualities and his poetical reputation; Ticknor because he was a stranger from the New World, and so on.

As we have seen, Almack's heyday of fashion and splendour lasted from its inauguration in 1765 till about 1835. At the end of that period signs were not wanting that its decay was at hand. The reasons for this are sufficiently obvious: the conditions of society were rapidly changing. With the accession of Queen Victoria an entirely new era was inaugurated—the fact that a female Sovereign held sway made it difficult for ladies of the aristocracy to sustain that leadership of fashion which did not clash with the royal prerogative while easy-going monarchs like George IV. and his brother governed the country. Some of the Lady Patronesses were, too, growing old; others, like Princess Lieven and Princess Esterhazy, had left England; and this helped to break up that clique which had ruled so powerfully. With the discontinuance of the regular balls, Almack's became generally known as Willis's Rooms; although long before the assemblies were given up, the conduct of the place had passed into the hands of Almack's nephew, Willis.

During the earlier years of the Victorian era, Willis's Rooms were used for occasional lectures, readings, dances and concerts. So far as the last named forms of entertainment were concerned, there had been a precedent, for the Lady Patronesses from time to time permitted concerts and balls to be given here for the benefit of fashionable professors of dancing and well-known musicians and singers. Here, from 1808 to 1810, Mrs Billington and Braham and Signor Naldi gave a series of concerts in opposition to those of Madame Catalini, at the Hanover Square Rooms; here M. Fierville gave his subscription balls, for which Bartolozzi engraved the beautiful little tickets; and in 1821 the Duc de Grammont, Envoy Extraordinary from France, gave here the splendid ball on the occasion of George IVth's Coronation, when the King, the Duke

PLATE 33

CELEBRITIES IN HYDE PARK: THE DUKE OF WELLINGTON,
MRS. ARBUTHNOT, PRINCE DE TALLEYRAND, AND COUNT D'ORSAY
From a Contemporary Print

THE DUKE OF WELLINGTON TAKING HIS MORNING RIDE IN THE ROW (1842)
From a Painting by H. de Danbrava

PLATE 34

BUCKINGHAM PALACE, FROM ST. JAMES' PARK (1842)
By T. S. Boys

GORE HOUSE, KENSINGTON, IN THE DAYS
OF LADY BLESSINGTON AND D'ORSAY
From a Drawing by T. H. Shepherd

of Wellington and a brilliant company were present and, according to Rush, each lady on entering the ball-room was presented with a beautiful bouquet.

In 1839 there appeared at Willis's Rooms one of the great army of remarkable prodigies—Master Bassie, aged thirteen, who, according to Thornbury, " appeared here in an extraordinary mnemonic performance." Five years later Charles Kemble gave his " Readings from Shakespeare " in the great ball-room ; in 1851 Thackeray here delivered his lectures on the English Humourists—the course extending, off and on, from May 22nd to July 3rd. Seldom, perhaps, had that "great painted and gilded saloon, with long sofas for benches," as Charlotte Brontë describes it, been filled, even in the heyday of its fashionable existence, by such an illustrious throng. Here were to be seen the authoress of " Jane Eyre " timidly exchanging greetings with Monckton Milnes and Lord Carlisle; here that amusing diarist, Caroline Fox, remarked Carlyle and Dickens and Leslie, besides " innumerable noteworthy people " ; here came the learned Hallam ; that " book in breeches," Macaulay ; and that very " blue " Harriet Martineau. Indeed, there was quite a furore for these lectures and all notable London attended them. Dickens never gave any of his readings here, but on two occasions presided at public dinners in the great room ; one being on February 14th, 1866, when he acted as chairman at the annual feast of the Dramatic and Musical Fund ; the other on June 5th, 1867, when he took the chair at the ninth anniversary Festival of the " Railway Benevolent Society."

But this is taking us beyond our period, and it need hardly be said that innumerable other functions have taken place in Willis's Rooms before they became, as they are to-day, the Auction Rooms of Messrs. Robinson and Fisher. There seems to have been a precedent for the present use of the rooms as a mart, for in 1837, Messrs. J. G. & G. A. Sharp sold there, " By order of the Trustees appointed by his Majesty for the Collection and Distribution of the Deccan Booty," some remarkable precious stones, including the famous Nassuck Diamond which weighed no less than $357\frac{1}{2}$ grains, and was of the purest water.

Besides the alterations to the great room and its contiguous apartments, radical changes have taken place during recent years on this property. Willis's Restaurant was here carried on for a period of prosperity, on the west side, next to Pall Mall Place. On the east side many small shops have been built, flanked at the end by the old-fashioned house which has formed for a number of years the headquarters of the Orleans Club. Little, therefore, remains of the original Almack's but its outer walls and the memories which are preserved in the literature of the long period during which it flourished.

A word about that literature will conveniently bring this chapter to a close. The chief work of fiction bearing on this particular theme, is itself entitled "Almack's."[1] It was published by Saunders and Otley, of Conduit Street, in 1827, and that it had some success is proved by the fact that at least three editions were called for. It was in the nature of a *Roman à Clef*. The dedication is something of a curiosity; it runs as follows:—

> To that most distinguished and despotic Conclave
> Composed of their High Mightinesses
> The Lady Patronesses of the Balls at Almack's,
> The Rulers of Fashion, the Arbiters of Taste,
> The leaders of Ton, and the Makers of Manners,
> Whose sovereign sway over " the world " of London has long been established on the firmest basis,
> Whose Decrees are Laws, and from whose judgment there is no appeal;
> To these important Personages, all and severally
> Who have formed, or who do form, any part of that Administration usually denominated
> The Willis Coalition Cabal
> Whether members of the Committee of Supply, or Cabinet Counsellors
> Holding seats at the Board of Control,
> The following pages are, with all due respect, humbly dedicated by an old subscriber.

The work consists of one of those pictures of fashionable life at which Thackeray and others have had their fling; and, as the title denotes, is nearly wholly concerned with the intrigues of matrons and *débutantes* to gain access to Almack's. Some time after its appearance a " key " to it was issued, and is said to have been compiled by no less a person than Benjamin Disraeli. The name of Disraeli reminds me that in some of his earlier novels the place

---

[1] In 1828 another novel entitled "Almack's Revisited," in 3 volumes, was published.

SOCIAL CENTRES

figures prominently. The young Duke, it will be remembered, " galloped with grace and waltzed with vigour " at his *début* there, on which occasion " his dancing was considered consummate " ; and a Lady Almack is one of the characters in " Vivian Grey." In the long list of those three volume novels of the twenties, thirties and forties of the last century—the works of Mrs. Moberley, John Mills, *et hoc omne genus*—Almack's occurs again and again. Thackeray makes Jeames de la Pluche " worl round in walce at Halmax " ; Tom and Jerry and Corinthian Tom found a sort of apotheosis of amusement there ; and the pencil of Robert Cruikshank has immortalised " the crowd of high-bred personages " among which they found themselves, and the gilded halls of the great Temple of Fashion itself (Plate 38).[1] As I have said, the memoirs and diaries of the period are full of allusions to Almack's and its patronesses and habitués, but, perhaps, after all, the best description of it is not in prose at all, but in verse—the verse of Luttrell—the verse of his " Advice to Julia " :

" There baffled Cupid points his darts
With surer aim, at jaded hearts ;
And Hymen, lurking in the porch,
But half conceals his lighted torch.
Hence the petitions and addresses
So humble to the Patronesses ;
The messages and notes, by dozens,
From their Welsh aunts and twentieth cousins,
Who hope to get their daughters in
By proving they are *Founders kin*."

And he adds :

" —all bow down—maids, widows, wives—
As sentenced culprits beg their lives,
As lovers count their fair one's graces,
As politicians sue for places ;"

concluding with this apostrophe :

" O ! Julia, could you now but creep
Incog. into the room and peep,
Well might you triumph in the view
Of all he has resigned to you !
Mark, how the married and the single

[1] Cruikshank, in his illustrations to Pierce Egan, gives also a picture of an East-end parody of the place, entitled All-max.

LIFE IN REGENCY AND EARLY VICTORIAN TIMES

In yon gay group delighted mingle !
Midst diamonds blazing, tapers beaming,
Midst Georges, stars and crosses gleaming,
We gaze on beauty, catch the sound
Of music and of mirth around ;
And Discord feels her surprise ended
At Almack's—or at least suspended."

By George Cruikshank.

CHAPTER IV.

GAMING AND GAMESTERS.

GAMBLING has no special period and no special country. It is as old as Time. Its votaries are to be found among all classes and in all lands. Nor has it any specialised form. It hangs attendant on a horse race or a game of cards ; on contests of skill and on the results of chance. It is inherent in human nature, and in spite of laws and protests will hardly, one supposes, ever get itself thoroughly eradicated from social life. At the same time there have been periods when a marked increase in this sort of amusement has been particularly observable, and in this country the closing years of the 18th century and the earlier ones of the 19th stand out as the heyday of the worship of the Goddess of Chance.

Those even but superficially acquainted with the subject, will not need to be reminded that one of the characteristic features of this period was the super-gambling that went on in the clubs, in semi-public resorts, and even in private houses. Laws were passed to combat the spread of the mania, a mania which almost recalls that of the South Sea Bubble at an earlier day. But such regulations are difficult of enforcement, and in their despite sums which appal us even in these times when we are used to think in colossal figures, were nightly lost at Crockford's and White's, by men, such as Fox, who were helping to rule the nation, or who if in opposition were criticising those engaged in that arduous task.

The fact is that gambling was regarded as part and parcel of the daily life of the man of fashion: Brummell was a noted example who, if he occasionally won immense sums, in the long run found himself a ruined and discredited man as a result of his devotion to the "board of green cloth." D'Orsay carried on this tradition, and there is little doubt that not so much his extravagance in dress, as his losses at the gaming table, was the real cause of the Gore House *débacle*.

There is always a kind of mystery surrounding the haunts of the gamester. Even in our own day the general public is not aware of the *locale* of certain gambling centres until a police raid reveals their existence, and we find that the sedate looking house we have so often passed has hidden behind its respectable frontage a " hell " known to its habitués and suspected by the authorities, but by these only. It need hardly be said that similar places existed during the great era of play; and those who, walking in St. James's Street, wonder at the little picturesque by-way, known as Pickering Place, are passing by one of these once famous haunts—a sample of many that existed in all parts of the Metropolis.[1]

But the same thoroughfare can produce a far more notable example in what is now the Devonshire Club, but which for many a year under its former title of Crockford's was the chief temple of gambling in the West-end, whose annals in this respect rival those of its opposite neighbour, White's, and whose chief priest, " The Fishmonger " as he was called, has left a name which will last while the records of fashion continue to be read.

William Crockford was the son of a fishmonger who kept the picturesque bulk-head shop close to Temple Bar, well-known from engravings of that part of the town. Although he assisted his father in his business, his heart was not in it, and he was accustomed to haunt the humble gambling establishments then existing in the neighbourhood. Later he became a book-maker and a member of Tattersalls. It is not definitely known when he first went to the West-end, but about the year 1824 he is found associated with one Josiah Taylor, as the joint proprietor of Watier's Club which under its original manager had been closed in 1819, and had subsequently been run by a set of black-legs, till Crockford and Taylor re-opened it as a hazard bank. The joint concern was not, however, of long duration, for after about a year Crockford left it, and seems to have formed a rival establishment in St. James's Street, not improbably at the corner of King Street, on the site of the St. James's Bazaar which he later (in 1832) caused to be erected. Be this as it may, it was in 1828 that he opened the famous club which had been designed by Wyatt. In the previous year Creevey records going to see " Crockford's new concern, which is magnificent and perfect in taste and beauty." The diarist adds that " for a suite of rooms, it is the greatest lion in England, and is said by those who know the palace at Versailles to be even more magnificent than that ! "

There is a long description in " Bentleys' Miscellany " of the

---

[1] Close by, on the site of the present Marlborough Club, in Pall Mall, there formerly existed another club famous for high play, which had a special room downstairs, known as the " Jerusalem Chamber " where money lenders used to interview such of the members as were in need of their monetary assistance. " London Clubs," by Ralph Nevill.

chaotic state of St. James's Street during the erection of this splendid club-house and an elaborate account of the glories of its internal decorations. In the basement a small cock pit was constructed, and this unusual adjunct still survives, although the passage which is said once to have existed, into Piccadilly—a ready means of escape on the appearance of Bow Street runners or police—has since been bricked up.

Everything was done on a scale of opulence and splendour which speaks, more than anything, for Crockford's acquaintance with human nature in its relations with gambling. The sums he expended on the structure and its decoration, on the furnishing, and on the cellar of wines were enormous. The moderate charges he made for the best possible fare (the great Ude was his principal chef), and the open-handed way in which he dealt with his *clientèle* all prove his consummate knowledge in this direction. When he died in 1844 he left a colossal fortune, and it was in one of Nash's splendid houses in Carlton House Terrace that he expired.

Although Crockford's was undeniably fashionable the fact that its members numbered from 1,000 to 1,200 shows that no undue exclusiveness was exercised; indeed, on its opening, we are told that " the most wealthy of the land enrolled themselves as members

"Crockford's," by George Cruikshank.

and every stripling of fashion fed on the hope of becoming sooner or later one of the elect." The annual subscription was £25, but it was money well spent, in one way, for it enabled anyone who could get in to feed better than anywhere else in London, and at cheaper rates, and although Ude was paid £1,200 a year he seems not to have been above catering for the most unexacting of appetites.

The chief attraction was Hazard, although other card games were played; and, indeed, it is recorded that on one occasion Lord Rivers (he was called " Le Wellington des joueurs ") lost £3,400 at whist at a single sitting; while at another time he dropped no less than £23,000 in one evening.

Crockford ran his establishment with the aid of a select and influential committee, and by an agreement with this body he was bound to put up nightly " during the sitting of Parliament " a bank of £5,000. Indeed, everything was done on a lavish scale, and it is said that the yearly expenditure on dice alone amounted to no less than £2,000; and during the first two seasons as much as £300,000 is credibly reported to have changed hands.

There is little doubt that Crockford was not only a remarkable manager of a gaming club, but also an extraordinary judge of character, and that he had made himself acquainted with the monetary position of all his clients. He was, says an authority, a walking Domesday Book " in which were registered the day and hour of birth of each rising expectant of fortune: he would tell with the nicest exactitude the rent-rolls of property in perspective, to what extent such rent rolls had been anticipated by apparent heirs, and what further encumbrances they would reasonably and securely bear." Hence the vast credits which he allowed some of the regular players, and incidentally the enormous amount he left at his death.

In 1840 he retired from the management, a millionaire, and four years later he died. Disraeli writing to his sister on June 12, 1840, says: " One great resignation has occurred. Last night Crockford sent in a letter announcing his retirement. 'Tis a thunderbolt and nothing else is talked of. 'Tis the greatest shock to domestic credit since Howard and Gibbs. Some members are twelve years in arrear of subscriptions. One man owed £700 to the coffee room; all must now be booked up. The consternation is general." Considering the length of time he was associated with the club and the character of its amusements, it speaks highly for Crockford that his honesty was never impugned nor his correct conduct of the place questioned. His personal influence on the club is proved by the fact that it did not long survive his decease, and it seems to have broken

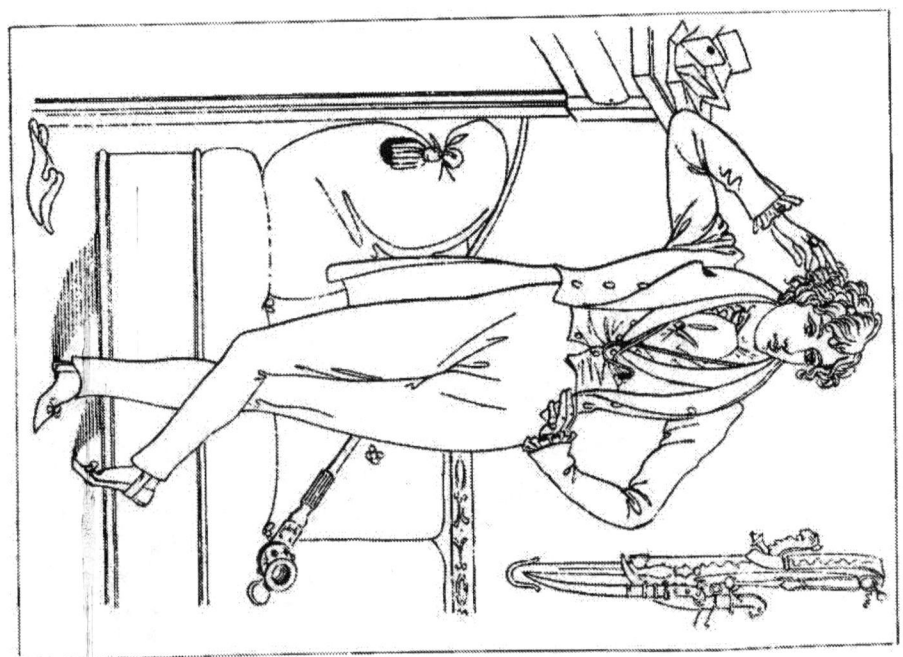
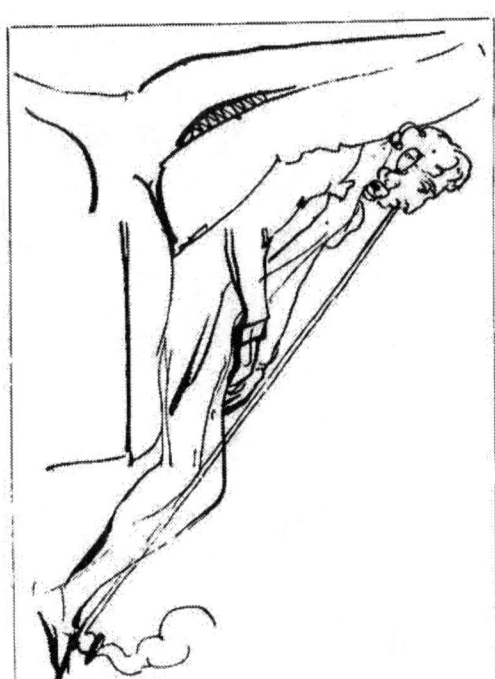

BENJAMIN DISRAELI (LEFT) AND BULWER LYTTON IN THE
DAYS OF GORE HOUSE
From Drawings by Maclise

CHISWICK HOUSE

From a Drawing by T. H. Shepherd

GAMING AND GAMESTERS

up about the year 1845.[1] Members were found to be using the place without paying their subscriptions; others even dared, in direct contravention of the Committee's law, to be seen smoking at the door!

In 1844 a Select Committee of the House of Commons sat to enquire into the state of the gaming laws, and to this committee Crockford was summoned, and gave evidence which is calculated to throw a curious light on the morality of certain phases of so-called sport. It is said that while this committee was still engaged on its labours, the police made a series of raids on no fewer than seventeen gambling hells all within a stone's throw of "Crockford's."

The other great headquarters of gambling in London at this period was White's, although, to be sure, there were many minor clubs whose excesses in this respect were only less because these centres were less important and smaller. White's Betting Book has become proverbial, but, of course, its startling pages only reveal those wagers which were based on passing events, and throw no special light on the regular gambling that went on in the card-rooms of the Club.

Although Brooks's, as we shall see, was a sort of rival to White's in gambling, as it was later to be in politics, the pre-eminence of the latter in this respect is largely due to the fact that Brummell, although he was also a member of Brooks's was, for many years White's special oracle. It was in 1798, on his leaving the Army in which he had served, if one can use the word in his connection, for but three years, that the Beau became a member, and from that time till his flight to the Continent in 1816, he ruled supreme there, and there occurred many of those incidents in his career which have passed into the anecdotage of the period. The famous Betting Book reveals various wagers laid by him on events of current interest and, rather pathetically, there occurs in its pages, under date of 1819, this entry: "Lord Yarmouth gives Lord Glengall four guineas to receive one hundred guineas if Mr. G. Brummell returns to London before Buonaparte returns to Paris."

During the last portion of the earlier half of the 19th century George Raggett ruled the destinies of White's, but for the first sixteen years of the period it was the decorative figure of Brummell,

---

[1] It is probable that from the time of his resignation in 1840 till his death in 1844, Crockford retained some kind of interest in the place, and in any case was at hand to be consulted on difficult points by the Committee.

together with those of his pet cronies, that dominated its card-room or appeared in their glory in its famous bow window. Although games of chance were largely indulged in, it must not be supposed that they monopolised the attention of the gaming set among the club members. Indeed, Gronow affirms that the play at Brooks's, for instance, was of a more hazardous character—faro and macao being the chief causes of the gaining or losing nightly of immense sums. But almost equally large were the losses at whist, of which White's was the headquarters. It is known that General Scott, Canning's father-in-law, won first and lost £200,000 at White's, through his skill at this game allied to a careful *régime* calculated to keep his brain clear and his wits alert. Brummell, too, was frequently a considerable winner, his greatest coup being the £20,000 he won in a single sitting from George Drummond, the Banker, on the one and only occasion on which the latter ever played whist at the club. Notwithstanding such isolated pieces of luck, it was gambling that brought about the Beau's downfall more surely even than did his quarrel with the Prince, and his waning popularity which resulted from that cause or from the influx into society of the men who had fought valiantly in the Napoleonic wars, and who helped to eclipse the glory of the effeminate lounger in St. James's Street.

There is no necessity to enter more fully into the annals either of White's or Brooks's, because both clubs have had their history ably recorded elsewhere[1]; but it may be mentioned that Brummell's successor as the leader of London fashion, D'Orsay, was never a member of either, nor was one of the most assiduous frequenters of Gore House, Prince Louis Napoleon—although it is known that the latter would have regarded election to White's as consolidating his position in the land of his exile, just as when, at a later date he was created a Knight of the Garter, he is said to have remarked, on leaving the historic hall where the ceremony took place : " Enfin je suis Gentilhomme."

Although gambling was prevalent in certain of the London clubs, it must be remembered that during the earlier years of the century those clubs were limited in number, for besides White's and Brooks's there were, not counting Crockford's, but five in the West-end : Boodles', Watier's, Arthur's, Graham's and the Guards'. The

---

[1] The History of White's by the Hon. Algernon Bourke, 2 vols., 1892 ; and Memorials of Brooks's 1764-1900, 1 vol., 1907.

GAMING AND GAMESTERS

opportunities for play were, therefore, much more restricted than would be the case to-day, if anything like the excessive gambling of the Regency times took place.

Most of the clubs here named were established before the period dealt with, and their gambling traditions—as in the cases of White's and Brooks's and Boodles' especially—had descended from an earlier generation. In some instances, although this was so, the present club-houses date from our period, as for instance Arthur's, which was built by a Mr. Hopper in 1825; and the Union, first started at Cumberland House in 1805, but migrating to its new home, built for it by Sir Robert Smirke, in 1824. Incidentally it may be mentioned that the Travellers was founded about 1832 when Barry designed its club-house, and that the Oriental (to which no doubt Joseph Sedley belonged) began its career in 1824, at 16, Lower Grosvenor Street; while the Carlton, started by the Duke of Wellington in 1831, in Charles Street, migrated to its headquarters in Pall Mall, built by Sir Robert Smirke, in 1836.[1]

But these latter and other clubs that will occur to the reader, cannot be termed gambling clubs, and are thus only indirectly connected with that subject in the way that any fraternity may be where card-playing is carried on. It is therefore Crockford's, White's and Brooks's (Plate 30), which we chiefly associate with the worship of the Goddess of Chance as it obtained in the West-end; and to these must be added two other centres: Watier's and Grahams's.

The former took its name from the famous cook attached to Carlton House. The story goes that at a dinner at the Prince Regent's table, the Prince enquired of some members of White's and Brooks's who were present, what sort of fare they got at their clubs, when Sir Thomas Stepney replied that it was always the same, solid but lacking variety and horribly monotonous. Upon this the Prince rang for Watier and, on his appearance, asked him if he would care to take a house and organize a club. Watier agreed, and named Madison, the Prince's page as manager, and Labourie as chief cook. No 81, Piccadilly, at the east corner of Bolton Street, was forthwith taken, and Watier's Club was started there in 1805-6. It soon became the greatest gambling club in London, and the appropriateness of its headquarters is proved by the fact that No.

[1] Wholly reconstructed by Sidney Smirke in 1854, and now re-faced.

81 had, at an earlier time, a particularly bad reputation as a "hell." Watier's was Brummell's own particular club; indeed, he is said to have had much to do with its inception; but at that time anything emanating, as this did, from Carlton House was regarded as being due to his influence. There is no doubt, however, that the beau reigned supreme there, "laying down the law in dress, in manners, and in those magnificent snuff-boxes, for which there was a rage; he fomented the excesses, ridiculed the scruples, patronised the novices, and excercised paramount dominion over all," according to Raikes, one of the members. The same authority tells some anecdotes bearing on this: how, for instance, Tom Sheridan once came into the club and, although not an habitual gambler, laid £10 at macao. Brummell happened to drop in from the Opera at the moment, and proposed that he should take Sheridan's place, promising to go half shares with him in any winnings he might receive. This being agreed to, for Brummell's luck at this particular game was notoriously phenomenal, the beau added £200 to his friend's modest stakes, and in ten minutes had won £1,500. Here he stopped and handing £750 to Sheridan remarked "There, Tom, go home and give your wife and brats a supper, and never play again." Another story also concerns Brummell at this club. One night his usual luck had deserted him and he lost a large sum, whereupon he affected, in his farcical way (it is Raikes who relates the story) a very tragic air, and called to the waiter: "Bring me a flat candlestick and a pistol." Upon which Bligh, an eccentric member, whose ways were the talk of the place, calmly produced two loaded pistols and exclaimed, "Mr. Brummell, if you are really anxious to put a period to your existence, I am extremely happy to offer you the means without troubling the waiter." As the narrator adds, "the effect upon those present may easily be imagined, at finding themselves in the company of a known madman who had loaded weapons upon him."

Watier's only lasted a little more than a decade. The pace was too rapid, and it died a natural death in 1819, from the paralysed state of its members. It brought ruin and death to many, but during the years of its prosperity, it must have been notable for the good breeding and humour of its members; although when Raikes states that these were never once interrupted by a personal quarrel, he seems to have forgotten a circumstance connected with himself which Gronow relates thus: Upon one occasion Jack

Society in Hyde Park (1842)

By T. S. Boys

PLATE 37

PLATE 38

Shopping in Bond Street (1823)   By W. Heath

Driving a Tandem! (1822)   By H. Alken

Dancing at Almack's (1822)   By G. Cruikshank

The Interior of a Large Shop: the Western Exchange, Old Bond Street, in 1817

From a Drawing by G. Smith

PLATE 39

PLATE 40

Buying a Horse at Tattersall's (1823)   By W. Heath

Racing a Tandem through the Country (1823)   By W. Heath

The Interior of a Cockpit: a Fight between a
Bulldog and a Prize Monkey (1822)   By H. Alken

GAMING AND GAMESTERS

Bouverie was losing large sums and became very irritable; Raikes with bad taste laughed at Bouverie, and attempted to amuse us with some of his stale jokes; upon which Bouverie threw his play-bowl, with the few counters it contained, at Raikes' head; unfortunately it struck him, and made the city dandy angry, but no serious results followed this open insult.

Readers of the amusing pages of Raikes and Gronow and other less well-remembered annalists of the day, will be able to add all sorts of anecdotes to these, for the clubs were then the centres where good things were said and repeated; and if all the acts of the members had been equal to so many of their recorded sayings, these coteries might well have been regarded as the best schools for the rising generation. Unfortunately it was quite otherwise, and Graham's, notable for its excessive and ruinous play, produced that famous scandal in which the bearer of an old and hitherto honoured name was the protagonist.[1] Graham's club-house was at 87, St. James's Street. It has been called the greatest of card clubs, and a long list would be required in which to set down the names of those of its members who retired from it broken, or who staved off the evil day by frequent applications to Messrs. Howard and Gibbs, the then fashionable and much patronised money-lenders. It was at Graham's that Lord Henry Bentinck is said to have invented the famous "Blue Peter" or call for trumps; here, too, Colonel Aubrey is once credibly reported to have lost £35,000; but as that gentleman once declared that next to winning, losing was the greatest pleasure in life, one supposes he found consolation in his *débacle*.

Apart from what took place in the clubs, gambling was carried on largely in more or less public gaming resorts (Plate 27), and although stringent laws were constantly being passed with a view to limiting it in such centres, the effect seems to have been to drive its votaries into those private hells which can only be reached by the somewhat complicated system of raids, and many of which possessed all sorts of contrivances for baffling the efforts of the authorities. As an instance of the severity with which gambling was dealt with when it was possible to bring off a coup, the case of the King v. Josiah Taylor, in the year 1825, may be cited. In this case the Court of King's Bench sentenced the defendant to pay no less a fine than £5,000, to be imprisoned in Clerkenwell Gaol for a year, at the

[1] The Satirist, a newspaper of the day, charged the peer in question with cheating. He brought an action for libel in which some very strange evidence was given, but losing it, went abroad and died in 1837.

expiration of which period he was to give security for good behaviour for another five years, himself in £10,000 with four other securities in £2,000 each. Such an exemplary sentence may be supposed to have given cause to keepers of public, and even to some extent, of private, gambling hells, and no doubt this was the case. But the mania for risking money, when in-bred in certain sections of society, as during this period it was to an abnormal degree, does not wholly depend on cards or a green table. Men betted on every conceivable subject, and the contemporary verses describing how some " Bucks," watching two drops of rain running down the club window immediately proceeded to lay wagers on which should arrive at the bottom first, but who were over-reached by the fact that the drops merged into each other before getting to the window-sill, well illustrates the trivial circumstances that were good enough to set *blasé* young men speculating as to how they could win one another's money.[1]

One reads in contemporary newspapers such items of intelligence as the following (March 28th, 1811): "The brother of a noble Marquis is said lately to have won at hazard upwards of £30,000, all in one night;" and again (April 3rd of the same year): "A young gentleman of family and fortune lost £7,000 on Sunday morning at a gaming house in the neighbourhood of Pall Mall." Most things got into the papers in those days when life was less complicated than it has since become, and these are but specimens of what went on, dished up in such a way as to be clear enough to those in the inner ring of Society, but sufficiently cryptic to tickle the palates of those who would like to have been. Those who ran large clubs like Crockford's, or who carried on more secret resorts, made a good thing out of the fool and his money; and certain old families still suffer from the doings of a Regency Buck among their forebears. But such vast centres as the Stock Exchange did not give facilities for winning or losing money to so many as has since been the case; and as the passion for play like the passion for drink seems to be inherent in human nature, so I suppose the gambling of this period was not much better or worse than what had occurred during earlier times and what, in a different way, has obtained more or less since.

I have said that gaming took place in more or less public resorts other than the clubs already alluded to, and it was there that the unwary stood the greatest risk of being swindled. In the clubs,

[1] "Fashion Then and Now," by Lord William Pitt Lennox.

LEADING IN THE DERBY WINNER

From a Contemporary Print

PLATE 41

PLATE 42

"Poringdale Oak," by John Crome

"Rouen," by R. P. Bonington

THE ENGLISH LANDSCAPE SCHOOL OF THE
EARLY NINETEENTH CENTURY

although large fortunes were made and lost, everything was done legitimately (if one can use the word in this connection) and above board; in the semi-public hells that abounded there was always the chance of a greenhorn becoming the victim of those *chevaliers de l'industrie* who abounded at this period.

It was in 1815 that the first establishment where the game of Rouge et Noir, just introduced from Paris, was set up in Pall Mall by a man named Roubel. Play began at two o'clock in the afternoon and continued till two or three o'clock in the morning. It is said that the expenses of this house amounted to over £8,000 a year, but the profits were so large that it was not long before other places of the same character came into existence—Fielden's at the north east corner of Bennett Street, St. James's, for example, and Taylor's at 57, Pall Mall.

Terrible stories are told of the direful effects of these temples of chance on their bewitched votaries. One may suffice, as an indication of many. It is thus recorded by a contemporary writer: " A well educated gentleman, well-known as Major B—, who was formerly in the Life Guards, and present at Waterloo, had, in the course of two or three years, lost at the *rouge et noir* tables the whole of his fortune; the proceeds of the sale of his commission followed; and lastly disappeared his valuable furniture, pictures and, in fact, everything he possessed. Thus reduced, he became a pensioner on the man whom his ruin had enriched; but this pittance being withdrawn, he fell into the lowest state of poverty and want. He was seen about town literally clothed in rags, and suffering from want approaching to starvation. His accumulated distress and misery compelled him to accept the wretched protection afforded by a parish workhouse." Even a worse fate than the workhouse resulted often enough from the gambling mania, and one might parody Johnson's lines, and say:

By George Cruikshank.

" There mark what ills the *gambler's* life assail,
    Toil, envy, want, the *workhouse*, and the gaol."

Chapter V.
ART AND LITERATURE, ETC,
ART

It is rather customary for the superior person to regard the art-movement of the first half of the 19th century in this country as one below criticism. In the polished academic mannerisms of certain exponents of pictorial representation, we are apt to overlook the great and outstanding work done in other directions of painting during this period ; and Landseer and Leslie too often make us forget Turner and Constable. As a matter of fact, with one exception, the years which elapsed between 1800 and 1850, witnessed developments in Art such as had not been dreamed of in England at an earlier day. The one exception was portraiture, in which direction, in spite of a few fine artists, there was a curious set-back from the glorious work done during the latter half of the 18th century ; and we shall seek in vain, except in one instance, for any real rivals of Reynolds, Gainsborough or Romney (to name but these three outstanding men) among the portrait painters of the period here dealt with.

On the other hand, landscape-painting entered on a phase of activity as glorious as it was to be suggestive. It has been usual to speak of Richard Wilson as the father of this branch of art, and there is no gainsaying the fact that he was the first to rescue landscape-painting from degeneracy, and from the perpetuation of that hard and tight method by which his predecessors and many of his contemporaries were shackled. But great as he relatively was, it was not to him but to his successors that we look as the real founders of this branch of art. Most of these great men ended their careers about the middle of the 19th century—De Wint died in 1849, and Turner, David Cox, Prout, Copley, Fielding, and Cotman within a few years of him—although Crome had ended his career in 1821 and Constable in 1837. That marvellous young man, Bonington, who was born in 1801, the year before Romney died, closed his short but pregnant career in 1828, and Patrick Nasmyth died three years later.

If we run over the illustrious names, it will be seen that what is best and greatest in English landscape painting, exercising that

ART

influence which the Barbizon school gratefully acknowledged, was the outcome of the period covering the first fifty or sixty years of the new century. To these such names as David Roberts, James Holland, Thomas Creswick, W. J. Müller and John Linnell, may be added, for although most of these artists outlived the fifties, their best work was being produced before then. The majority of these men were not Londoners, but the greatest of them was, for Turner, who was born in Maiden Lane in 1775, closed his busy life in 1851 at the little house in Chelsea, which happily still exists, watching from its roof the silvery lights on the Battersea reach.

But, as I have said, if English art reached its *apogée* at this time in the direction of landscape painting, it cannot truthfully be said to have shone equally conspicuously in that of portraiture. Perhaps the most notable exponent of this branch of the art was Sir Thomas Lawrence, who died in 1830, and who has left us a mass of work curiously unequal in merit, and whose claims to be considered a pre-eminent craftsman are still questioned by many. That he produced some masterpieces cannot be gainsaid; but he was a fashionable and busy man, and over-facility and a lack of self-criticism resulted in the throwing off of much work marked by a certain meretricious excellence, but hardly convincing us that it was the production of a really great artist.

Sir Martin Archer Shee was another fashionable portrait painter of the period (he died in 1850), who succeeded Lawrence as President of the Royal Academy, but whose work was of an even inferior calibre to that of his predecessor, and who, had he not possessed many social and literary qualifications, would probably not have attained the success he did as a painter. Both Hoppner and Opie, although they died respectively in 1810 and 1807, must be regarded as belonging to the foregoing century, and such men as Pickersgill, Sir George Hayter, Sir William Beechey, Jackson[1] and others represented, together with the much royally-patronised foreigner Winterhalter, the best that was being done in portrait painting during this rather arid period. One great name, however, must not be forgotten—that of Raeburn (his career closed in 1823), because Raeburn stands in the very fore-front of portrait painting, and as a delineator of men equalled Sir Joshua and Gainsborough and surpassed all other British portraitists.

[1] The name of Downman who survived till 1824, should be mentioned because of the beautiful portraits, heightened in colour, which he produced; but he is really an 18th century man.

LIFE IN REGENCY AND EARLY VICTORIAN TIMES

Many people who could not afford the prices (small as they relatively were) charged by the fashionable portrait painters, but who yet desired representations of themselves or their families, patronised those journeymen of art who produced the terrible effigies to be met with in so many homes to-day—pictures lacking in everything which goes to make such an object a thing of beauty, and probably lacking in the chief essential of a portrait, that of being a good likeness.

There were one or two reasons for the temporary eclipse of portrait painting as a branch of really great art. The development of the silhouette, a curious form of portraiture which had been invented by Etienne de Silhouette, in the 18th century, enabled many to obtain, at comparatively little cost, a form of representation—shadowy profile studies—which did better than nothing. Men, too, like Count D'Orsay, occupied themselves in drawing pencil sketches, mostly in profile, which had a fashion and which, although in a rather amateurish way, are not negligible as artistic objects and are certainly valuable as personal records. Daniel Maclise in his Fraser portraits, slight in outline, but carefully, sometimes beautifully, drawn, and excellent as likenesses, and Dighton and H. B. (Doyle), with their well-known caricature portraits, went a step further. But it was the invention by Daguerre and Niepce of the photograph (daguerreotypes, as they were first called) in 1839, and the development of the calotype process by Fox Talbot in 1841, which hit portrait-painting hard as a paying art for many a year; for although it was not till after our period that photography really made those advances which have brought it almost within the realms of art, the novelty became fashionable, and for every early Victorian photograph that has come down to us some proportion of oil-portraiture has been lost.

But portrait painting has always been a sheet anchor in this country to the striving artist; such men as Chantrey (Plate 43) began with it; and Constable produced quite a number of pictures in this direction, while Haydon tore himself away from his beloved historical painting to bring grist to the mill by excursions into what to him seemed an alien and derogatory form of artistic achievement.

The name, by the bye, of this extraordinary man bulks largely during the earlier years of the 19th century. There is no more pathetic story than that of his life and aims. His great object was

W. M. Thackeray
From a Painting by S. Lawrence

Sir Francis Chantrey
From a Drawing by Himself

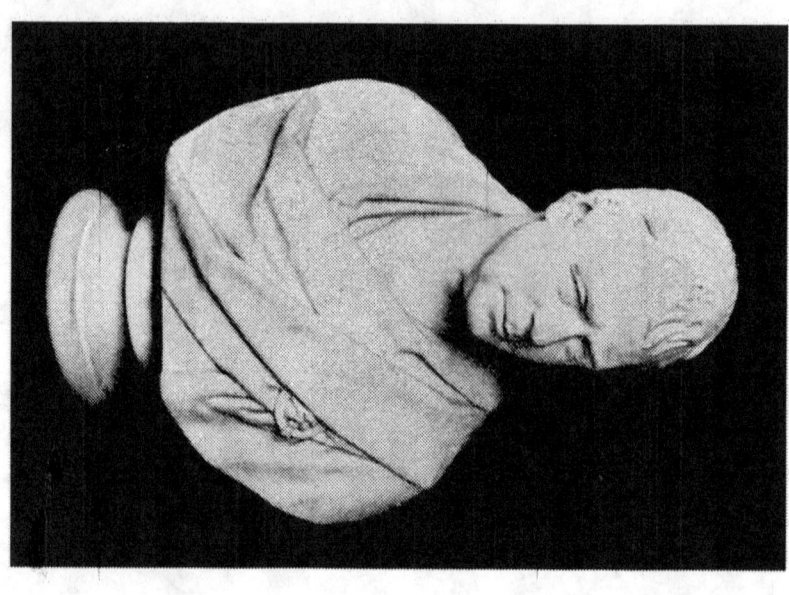

Bust of Sir Walter Scott
By Sir F. Chantrey

J. M. W. Turner
From a Drawing by J. Phillip (1850)

to form a school of Historical Painting. He suggested the decoration of the House of Lords, and when it was carried he was not among those selected for the work; he tried to induce the authorities to order an altar piece for each of the new churches that were about to be erected during the early years of the century; he urged the filling of the Royal Exchange with frescoes, and he died by his own hand, a disappointed man, before anything was done. He had, however, his great and even glorious moments. You can read about them in that most entertaining and delightful book any artist has ever written—his "Autobiography and Journals." All his colossal pictures are forgotten— his "Dentatus," his "Urial," his "Satan," and his "Napoleon" and the rest. But his megalomania, his perpetual monetary difficulties, his intense enthusiasm, his genius for descriptive writing, will survive as long as those self-revealing diaries are read. Haydon was a man of genius with that touch of madness to which all genius is more or less allied; but his genius (and how amazed he would be, poor fellow, to hear it stated) did not lie in painting.

Fuseli was another man of not dissimilar mental calibre, although a much better craftsman, whose life extended till 1825, and who in 1804 had been made keeper of the Royal Academy. His writings, consisting of the Lectures he delivered, which had an undoubted influence on the art of his day, have, too, survived his pictorial work—although the latter is not so unknown as is that of Haydon, being represented both in the National Gallery and at Liverpool. So far as literary success goes Northcote is much in the same boat: his "Conversations" still making fascinating reading; while who knows his pictures?

To these may be added the names of Barry, who died in 1806, and whose vast splashings fill the Lecture Room of the Society of Arts; Hilton (1786-1839), whose "Ganymede" is in the Diploma Gallery; Benjamin West, academic and ephemeral[1]; and William Blake—that extraordinary man who lived in a spiritual as well as a material world, and whose "dreams" and "visions" have been the wonder and the enigma of our day.

Rather later there arose a school of "genre" painters who gave themselves to the rendering of domestic scenes, as did Wilkie

[1] His Annunciation, which occupied from 1817 to 1826, a position in Marylebone Church, brought him £800; in 1840 it was sold for £10. This might induce us to think that art criticism was on the upward grade, but I fear it was only due to a change in fashion.

and Mulready and Collins, or to the recording of scenes from the classics, as did C. R. Leslie, Maclise, E. M. Ward, and Frith, in his earlier and better days. Landseer's academic style suited those who liked the " polished " follower of Snyders and Oudry; and Etty was a revelation in flesh-painting; while Callcott and Eastlake *et hoc omne genus*, were considered outstanding men, before the appearance of a greater school with more enlarged views and with a greater sense of " values."

It is impossible to mention a tithe of the painters who flourished during the first half of the century. The reader who is interested in this branch of progress, will himself be able to fill up the large gap. But in a lesser direction of art—that of illustration—some really great names must not be omitted. The beginning of the century saw the rise of George Cruikshank, who lived on till our own day. The importance to us here of Cruikshank lies not so much in that series of plates which he executed for the works of Dickens, Harrison Ainsworth, and the rest, as for what he did, in an hundred other directions, in his Comic Almanacks, his " Omnibus," etc., etc., to depict and preserve pictorially the manners and customs and the dress of the period. There was always something rather impish and exaggerated in his work, but it possesses the fundamental value of being a record whose importance it is impossible to overestimate. Another man of whom much the same may be said, although his methods were so different, was " Dicky " Doyle, the son of the famous " H.B.," who should be known to everyone, if for nothing else, because he produced that illustrated cover for Punch (started in 1841) which is familiar all over the world. But besides his " Bird's-eye view of Society," his " Mr. Pipys, His Diary," etc., give us those revealing pictures of the life of London which, although, like the works of his great contemporary Leech, they appeared towards the close of the period covered by this book, yet essentially recorded the habits of the Londoner during the earlier years of the Victorian era, and have stamped them on our mind's eye better than pages of mere description could do.[1]

The names of other outstanding illustrators will spring automatically to the memory. Seymour who began to illustrate Pickwick, but who committed suicide before he had gone very far; Buss, his very inadequate successor; and Hablot K. Brown (Phiz), whose name

---

[1] Rowlandson and Gillray lived well into the century, but they must be considered as 18th century artists.

ART

is linked up with those of Boz and Lever, as the pictorial companion of their journeys through the green and pink covered parts of their novels. Thackeray, too, who illustrated his own yellow covered *fascicules*, and wanted to adorn the pages of Pickwick, should not be forgotten, because although as an artist he was lacking in all sorts of essentials, yet he contrived to give that air of the period to his plates which better craftsmen had often failed to do.

The period of the great miniature painters—the Cosways, Englehearts, Humphreys and the rest—had passed with the passing of the 18th century, but there were one or two exponents who, if not comparable with such as these, still did good work and are not yet forgotten. Of these the best known is Ross, who was a pupil of another once fashionable miniaturist, Andrew Robertson, and who with Chalon divided the honours of such work and became a favourite not only with the Court but also with the public. Chalon, an equally popular master of the art of painting " in little," did not believe that photography would replace miniature. Once Queen Victoria hinted to him her fears in this respect: "Oh, Madame," he replied, "there is no danger, photography does not flatter." Both Chalon and Ross lived till 1860, and although there was a variety of lesser people engaged in this special branch of art— was not Miss La Creevy one of them, perhaps the best remembered— the art may be said to have died with them; for notwithstanding that, more or less recently, there has been an attempt to resuscitate it, and many brilliant miniaturists are working to-day, it is probable that it will never again be widely popular, as it was in the days before Daguerre and Niepce came and dealt it, *pace* Chalon, its death-blow.

That there was a movement towards a better understanding and appreciation of art generally during this period is obvious in many ways. The writings and lectures of Hazlitt (who died in 1830) drew attention not only to the literature but to the art of the past; Ruskins' first volume of modern painters appeared in 1843, and his " Seven Lamps " (" Gas-lamps, Seven," as Kingsley irreverently called them) came out six years later; and although it has become the fashion nowadays to forget Hazlitt and depreciate Ruskin, there is no doubt that the influence of these two men, their knowledge, their powers of embodying their opinions in beautiful and forcible English, and their tremendous earnestness, made a great and, in certain directions of their teaching, a lasting impression. The writings, too, of such authorities as Waagen, Mrs. Jameson, and a host of others who dealt with art in a literary way, gave an impetus which resulted in a more general attention being given to the subject.

Added to these influences, sometimes arising out of them, may be mentioned the formation of those great art galleries which were once the glory of London, but many of which have since been dispersed to the four winds. The National Gallery was begun in 1824, and by the gradual accumulation, often through gift, of such collections as the Beaumont (in 1826), the Carr (in 1831), the Olney (in 1837), the Farnborough (in 1838), and the Vernon (in 1847), formed the nucleus—added to in 1856 by Turner's great bequest—of that assemblage of pictures of which Ruskin once said that " for the purpose of the general student it was the most important collection of paintings in Europe."

The Marquises of Hertford were busy during this period in accumulating those wonders which are to-day the Nation's glorious legacy in the Wallace collection ; the fruits of his campaigns may be seen in the gallery which the great Duke assembled at Apsley House ; the Duke of Bridgwater and Lord Gower purchased the famous Orleans collection, and thus formed the nucleus of the inestimably rich gallery at Bridgwater House, and of many of those pictures which were once at Stafford House. Other London mansions, and many a country seat were being filled by their owners with pictures of the old masters ; and there were certain men like Lord Egremont, Lord Lansdowne, Samuel Rogers, and others who patronised contemporary art as well as that of the past. Many of these seem to have exercised less judgment in their purchase of the works of living artists than they did in the collection of paintings of earlier schools. Much done in this way was obviously due to charitable motives (Haydon's journals are full of the records of such things, although Haydon never doubted but that he gave more than he got, and was systematically underpaid), and when we smile at some " horror " hanging amid real works of art we must remember this, and recognise that probably the heart of the patron dominated his head.

Other influences were at work. The Society of Dilletanti helped by its patronage such travellers as Sir William Gell, in bringing to this country specimens of the remains of classic art ; men like Nollekens and Hamilton were purveying from calmly regardless lands, antiquities which to-day may be seen in our national, and in many

SYDNEY SMITH
From a Painting by H. P. Briggs

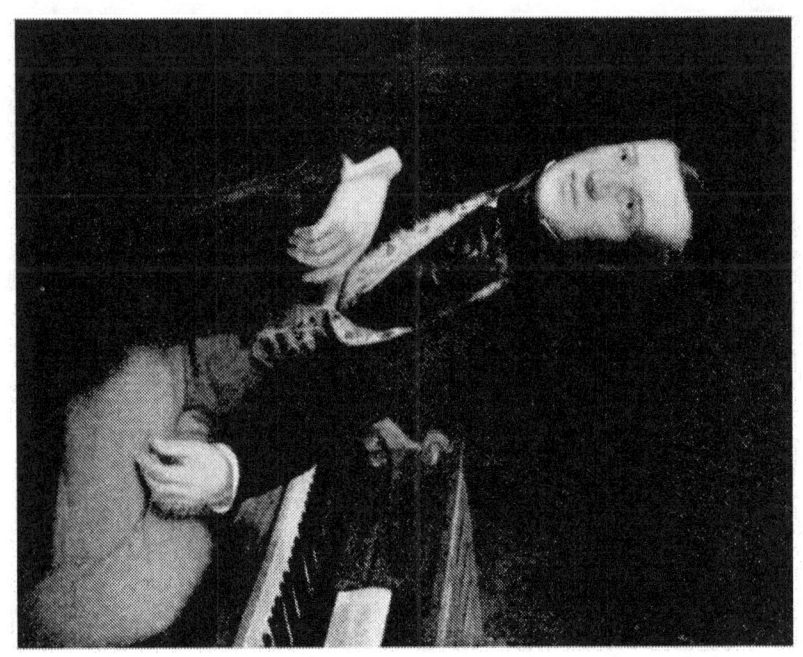

MICHAEL WILLIAM BALFE
From a Painting by R. Rothwell

PLATE 45

PLATE 46

A Meeting of the Royal Society (1807)
By *William Walker*

A Dinner to the Dilettanti Society
at the Thatched House Club (1841)
By *T. H. Shepherd*

a private, collection. The Royal British Institution was only second to the Royal Academy in its services towards the promotion of British Art and in the premiums given to artists. The opening of the Royal Hibernian Society in 1825, and the Royal Scottish Academy a few years later, helped to extend the love and acceptance of art.

In another direction—that of Architecture—great advances in general recognition were made, and by the establishment in 1831 of the Architectural Society, and that of the Royal Institute of British Architects, six years later, an official imprimatur was given to this phase of Art, in which the names of Soane and the Smirkes, Decimus Burton, Nash and Barry, with what they achieved in the London of 1800-1850, are outstanding.

Other artistic societies at this period were the Royal British Artists, inaugurated in 1823; the School of Design at Somerset House, opened under Government auspices, in 1837; and the Society for Promoting Practical Design; while the Society of Painters in Water Colours which first opened its doors at 20, Lower Brook Street, in 1808, gave place to a new society of the same name, whose initial exhibition was held at 16, Old Bond Street, in 1832, under the auspices of men whose names are household words as *aquarellistes* and whose efforts raised this branch of the fine arts in England to an unassailable eminence—Copley Fielding, De Wint, Harding, W. Hunt, G. Barrett, and others too numerous to mention in this brief survey.

There was one other great incentive to the art movement of this period, affecting all branches of it, but chiefly appealing to sculpture, the acquisition of the famous Elgin Marbles which had been brought from Greece by Lord Elgin in 1815, and sold to the Nation, in the following year, for £35,000. These marvellous relics of antiquity, and glorious examples of the sculptor's art at its greatest period, were added to the Hamilton and Townley collections (purchased in 1805-11) and formed a gallery of plastic art whose influence on the sculptors of the period—Flaxman, the Westmacotts, Gibson, Chantrey, Wyatt, Behnes, Foley, Macdowell, and Baily, can hardly be exaggerated.[1]

[1] The name of Baxter, the inventor of the colour-printing which bears this title, ought not to be forgotten. His work was rather in the form of a commercial medium for art, but his process led the way to developments and to attention being paid to the possibilities of colour production. Besides this, his little pictures have become rare and are to-day sought after, and thus have an interest which their actual artistic claims would hardly warrant.

LIFE IN REGENCY AND EARLY VICTORIAN TIMES

LITERATURE

To deal with the literature of the first half of the 19th century, in anything like an adequate way, would require a volume—so full is it in its output, so far-reaching in its influence and effects. In no way does the transition stage at which we had arrived during this period show itself more markedly than in the changes that came over literary achievement. The years that saw the close of that great era in which Scott and Keats, Coleridge and Lamb, flourished, witnessed also the beginning of that equally pregnant period when Dickens and Thackeray, Tennyson and Browning, were the literary planets, and when Wordsworth carried on the traditions of an earlier day, and linked up the Victorian age with that of the Regency. Between the beginning of the century and the accession of Queen Victoria, births and deaths had given to or taken from the British literary world some of its outstanding figures. Sheridan died in 1816, a purely Georgian figure; Jane Austen in the following year; Keats and Shelley expired prematurely a few years later, and Byron in 1824; while Scott and Crabbe, Lamb and Coleridge, survived till the thirties. But the lamp was being caught up by other hands; Tennyson and Elizabeth Browning were born in 1809; Lytton in 1803; Disraeli in 1804; Thackeray seven years later, and Dickens and Browning in 1812; while George Eliot's date is 1812, and that of Matthew Arnold ten years later. Two outstanding men who were born in the preceding century lived on throughout our period—Wordsworth and Carlyle; Macaulay (1800-1859) set the seal to his fame by the publication of the first two volumes of his History, a year before the half century was reached.

It need hardly be said, for it will be sufficiently obvious to those with only a limited knowledge of the literary history of the period, that these names are but a very few, although they are the most illustrious, of that band of authors which made the periods of the Regency and of Victoria notable. But they serve as landmarks, and, besides, the majority of them were not only closely connected with London, but were figures in London society at a period when the Dandies ruled supreme, and the rather unusual spectacle was exhibited of great writers posing successfully as beaux, and competing with men of leisure and fashion, in the cut of a coat and the conduct of an eye-glass.

LITERATURE

We all know how proud Goldsmith was of his plum coloured suit fresh from Filby's; had some of his literary successors been equally simple in their confessions we should find, I have no doubt, that Thackeray was as pleased with his appearance at Lady Blessington's, and that Dickens took as much pains over the selection of those wondrous decorated waistcoats which he wore, as over the incidents which crowded the pages of "Pickwick" and "Nickleby," "Vanity Fair," and "Esmond."

Many of the portraits of these illustrious men show them garbed in the dress of fashion, and Lytton and Harrison Ainsworth, Dickens and Thackeray and Disraeli (Plate 35), might be taken for specimens of the dandies of the day quite as much as Brummell and Alvanley and D'Orsay. And they not only appear in this pictorial form; their names are prominent in great assemblies, where their appearance created something like a sensation.

We, living in a time when life is crowded and complex, can hardly understand how a mere man of letters, however eminent, could be regarded as anything but a literary machine—to be heard and not seen. Not that the Court in those days, any more than in our own, extended any special recognition to writers—unless perhaps they happened to be foreigners. True, Sir Walter was a welcome guest at Carlton House, but then the Prince of Wales was notoriously un-select in his company. Once, too, towards the close of his life, Dickens, after he had become a world-famous figure, was honoured by an invitation to Buckingham Palace; while one hears of Carlyle, in his old age, meeting the Queen, in a surreptitious sort of way, at a tea at Dean Stanley's. Tennyson was in this respect a *persona grata* and read, in after years, his "In Memoriam" to his Sovereign, as all who know Max's delightful caricature of the incident are aware. But one never hears of Thackeray being invited to the Palace, or George Meredith or the Brownings. On the other hand Society, limited and select as it then was, does seem to have extended a welcome to those who were helping to make the age notable; and in the diaries and similar records of that period one comes across the names of many of these writers, and they take their places in the annals of fashion almost as prominently as they do in those of literature. Holland House would lose half its interest if we were bereft of Macaulay's delightful word pictures of its vie intime; Gore House and Lansdowne House and Devonshire House would all lack something, if the names of Thackeray and Dickens, Ainsworth, Landor, Disraeli, and the rest, were erased from the roll of their *habitués*.

During the earlier portion of our period the later works of Madame D'Arblay, or those of Jane Austen and the best of Maria Edgeworth, Susan Ferrier, Miss Mitford and Mrs. Gaskell, with the perennial splendour of Scott's genius playing like a lambent flame over all, formed the chief prose literary food of the time, interspersed with numbers of those old novels which may perhaps still be met with in circulating libraries with a past, making us (forgetful of the stacks of similar rubbish published to-day) wonder at the critical perception that could away with such very small beer. It was a time, too, when *romans à clef* had a vogue, and when such books as " Almacks " and its congeners excited an interest quite other than literary or critical.

In poetical achievement it was a wonderful period ; there was Scott, before he had embarked on his glorious succession of romances, and Byron who awoke to fame in St. James's Street, and whose " Don Juan" and "The Waltz" scandalised so many in a generation which one would have thought to be inured to such audacities. There was, too, that " Lake " school which infuriated the more sophisticated section of the public, and the " Cockney " School which maddened so many a reviewer.

The fact is the country was not worthy of the good things which were set before it. Its taste was vitiated, and a society that found Rogers a great poet and the Hon. William Spencer readable, could hardly be supposed to realise the splendour of Keats and Shelley or the real greatness underlying the frequent puerilities of Wordsworth. Lamb's exquisite critical discernment and inimitable style were recognised, but by relatively few ; while the marmoreal splendour of Landor's " Conversations " was above the heads of all but an esoteric coterie.

At a moment when the romanticism of Scott and his followers was being succeeded by the jejune efforts of third and fourth rate novelists, a young man was beginning his tentative efforts in what may be termed domestic fiction, in the pages of the " Evening Chronicle " and the " Monthly Magazine," and the " Sketches by Boz " came into existence, to be followed closely by Pickwick, and that series of novels which are, perhaps, better known throughout the world than any other works—the Bible and Shakespeare excepted.

LITERATURE

It would be impossible to exaggerate the impatience with which those monthly " green leaves " were awaited. The obvious disadvantage of reading novels on the instalment plan does not seem to have struck contemporaries ; and from 1837 till the moment when the magician was struck down in 1870, the public received with avidity those " parts " in which, with a few exceptions, Dickens's works appeared. The fashion for such a method of publication was in the air, and Thackeray and Lever and others followed with the yellow and pink leaves which have now become *desiderata* to the collector.

Dickens's first great success was in 1837 ; just ten years later Thackeray scored his initial hit with " Vanity Fair " ; while in the interval Lever, by the aid of " Harry Lorrequer," " Charles O'Malley," and " Tom Burke of Ours," secured the suffrages of a section of the public that delighted in the rollicking fun of the genial Irishman. Those were the days before psychological analysis came to trouble our minds ; when the object of a novel was to amuse, not to depress ; before the young lions of the nineties made a cult of dreariness, and revelled in misery. Hence, no doubt, the general acceptance of these great works. Thackeray's so-called cynicism was but skin-deep, and there was as much to amuse as to discourage in his pictures of life. And, above all these men could portray character ; their plots might be weak, as they so often were, their grammar might not have always been up to sixth form standard (although I shall be glad to come across a writer of clearer, more forcible, easier, more distinguished prose than Thackeray's at his best), but they knew a man or woman when they saw them, and if, as Dickens invariably did, they sometimes exaggerated external characteristics, their portraits were the more telling, just as a caricature often gives a better impression of its subject than a photograph.

It is clearly impossible to enter into even the most superficial survey of the literature of the period, in other directions. Carlyle and De Quincy were furthering the knowledge of German literature, which Coleridge had also helped to popularise ; while the " Opium Eater " appeared in 1822, and " Sartor Resartus " in 1833. Landor and Leigh Hunt, Southey and Sydney Smith and the " Edinburgh " set were all, *inter multos alios*, doing work in various ways, and linking up the earlier with the later portion of the period. The " Edinburgh " and the " Quarterly " came into existence during the first decade of the century ; the " Westminster Review "

LIFE IN REGENCY AND EARLY VICTORIAN TIMES

followed in 1824; and "Blackwood," "Fraser," "Bentley" and "The New Monthly," laid the foundations of those reviews which have since been succeeded by so many similar publications. Encyclopædias were much in vogue, too, and the names of men like Lord Brougham and Lardner (at whom Thackeray loved to tilt) are associated with such short cuts to knowledge.

Konig's principle of printing by steam gave an impetus to the Daily Press, and in 1814 "The Times" set up cylinders in Printing House Square, while by 1827 an improved machine, invented by Cowper and Applegath, with four cylinders, printed off 5,000 copies of the paper in an hour—then considered a remarkable achievement. A simpler system of inking subsequently came into force, and by 1848 further improvements resulted in the trebling of the output—an output that in these days seems small enough.

MUSIC

There are two other phases of life—bearing directly on manners and customs, which must at least be alluded to—Music and the Drama

As a matter of fact we relied chiefly on imported talent in this respect, and it was almost solely in glees, with Dr. J. W. Callcott as their chief exponent, that we could be said to have shown any special musical originality during the earlier years of the century. Dr. Crotch, who died in 1848, also did good work in this direction, although he shone chiefly as a composer of church music. He held the chair of music at Oxford till his death, when he was succeeded by Sir Henry Bishop, who was a most prolific writer in all sorts of styles and who, when he died in 1855, left no fewer than 82 operas, although it is by some of his beautiful songs that he is, to-day, chiefly remembered. Other names that will occur to the reader are those of John Hatton, whose opera, "Pascal Bruno," once had a success, and who was born in 1809; John Barnett, his contemporary, born in 1802, and E. J. Loder (1813-65). Then there was John Field, who composed in the manner of Chopin, although it is interesting to remember that he was born twenty-seven years before the great Polish composer, and that there seems little doubt that the latter took his nocturnes as models. Many more names could be added but they belong to forgotten men. There are, however, three British composers who are still remembered; Balfe

PLATE 47

MDME. CATALANI   MDME. PASTA
PRIMA-DONNAS OF THE EARLY '30's
From Drawings by A. E. Chalon

AN ENTR'ACTE AT COVENT GARDEN (1822)
By G. Cruikshank

PLATE 48

A Stage Spectacle at Sadler's Wells Theatre (1809)
By Rowlandson & Pugin

A Masquerade at the Restored "Pantheon" (1809)
By Rowlandson & Pugin

PLATE 49

THE KING LIGHTED TO THE ROYAL BOX (1824)
By Theodore Lane

THE GREEN ROOM AT DRURY LANE (1822)
By G. Cruikshank

KEAN AS KING RICHARD; ROYALTY IN THE BOX (1823)
By W. Heath

"THE GIG SHOP; OR KICKING UP A BREEZE AT NELL HAMILTON'S HOP"
By T. Rowlandson

A MILLING MATCH BETWEEN CRIBB AND MOLYNEUX (1811):
THE KNOCK-OUT
By T. Rowlandson

MUSIC

(Plate 45), Vincent Wallace and Sterndale Bennett. The former two were born in Ireland—Balfe at Dublin in 1808, and Vincent Wallace at Waterford in 1814. "The Bohemian Girl" of Balfe, and the "Maritana" of Wallace, were exceedingly popular in their day, and many of their charming arias are still remembered. Sterndale Bennett was born at Sheffield in 1816, and his "May Queen," perhaps his most attractive work, was produced at Leeds in 1858.

Of Henry Smart, the eminent organist and composer, who was born in 1813; of Samuel Wesley (nephew of the famous John), the composer of sacred music, who died in 1837; of William Crotch, who was something of an infant prodigy and had astonished Dr. Burney in this respect, and who died in 1847, it is only necessary to be thus allusive; while the name of John Hullah, as a technical exponent of the art, and those of Jullien and Costa, as conductors who attracted crowds as Sir Landon Ronald and Sir Henry Wood do to-day, should not be forgotten.

But as usual with England, it was, so far as executants were concerned, imported talent, as exemplified chiefly in Opera, that chiefly attracted the public, and if Mrs. Billington, and Braham were native products they were almost alone amid such as Madame Grassini, Angelica Catalani (Plate 47), Vestris (a grand-daughter, by the bye, of Bartolozzi, the engraver), Fodor, Pasta (Plate 47), Sontag, Malibran, Grisi, Lablache, Mario and, perhaps greater than all, Jenny Lind, who created such a *furore* that its memory has not yet entirely died away—a *furore* only equalled by that of the appearance of Paganini, whose almost diabolical cleverness amazed his generation and has become a legendary tradition.[1]

The Londoner of the period had, too, opportunities of seeing and hearing many of those great masters whose names are for ever inscribed on the roll of musical fame. If none of them lived, as Handel had done, in our midst for any length of time, they paid visits to this country as Hadyn and Mozart had at an earlier period. Louis Spohr first came here in 1820, when he stayed at 1a, Devonshire Street, Portland Place, and London was as astonished at his power over the violin as it was at the red waistcoat which he sported when about to be introduced to the directors of the Philharmonic Society. It was, of all places, at the "Hoop and Horseshoe" on Tower Hill, that Wagner spent the first night of his arrival in England,

[1] For word pictures of the Opera, with the Dandies and Lady Patronesses of Almack's as *arbitres elegantiarum*; see Gronow, Grantley Berkeley, etc.

LIFE IN REGENCY AND EARLY VICTORIAN TIMES

in 1839. Thirteen years earlier Weber had come over as the guest of Sir George Smart, at 103, Great Portland Street, and there, only a few weeks later, he died. Still other illustrious musical visitors were Mendelssohn, who on his first arrival here lodged at 79, Great Portland Street, where he was destined to stay on three subsequent occasions. There is extant a quite clever sketch of the river, showing St. Paul's, which he made on one of his visits, and the story of how, returning from a solemn diplomatic dinner, he and two friends saw some German sausages twopence each, and having bought some proceeded to eat them amid the conventional respectability of Portland Street, has been recorded by the great composer himself. Yet another visitor was Chopin, who was here on several occasions, the first being in 1837, when he stayed at 10, Bentinck Street, removing subsequently to 48, Dover Street, where he had three pianos—a Broadwood, an Erard and a Pleyel, and where, as he himself once said, his days passed like lightning. On a later visit he put up at 4, St. James's Place, for which lodging he paid "$4\frac{1}{2}$ guineas a week, inclusive of bed, coals, etc." This was in 1848, and it was on July 7th of that year that he gave a concert at Lord Falmouth's—No. 2, St. James's Square—of which an advertisement in the "Times" gives details.

Such centres as Mr. Attwood's house at Norwood, and Messrs. Broadwood's premises in Great Pulteney Street, are closely associated with these visits of musical celebrities; while the Argyll Rooms, Exeter Hall, the Hanover Square Rooms, and (which is so often forgotten) Crosby Hall, re-echoed to the strains of their works, and often to their actual performances. If you wander among the tombstones, too, of Kensal Green you will find there the resting place of many of those who, during the earlier part of the 19th century, charmed London with the concord of sweet sounds.

THE THEATRE

In the first chapter I made a rapid reference to the chief theatres that existed in London during our period, so that there is no necessity to go over the ground again. But a few words must be said concerning the notable actors and actresses who appeared at Drury Lane, Covent Garden, and elsewhere in London during

THE THEATRE

the half century. Especially is this essential, because it was a time of great importance so far as the stage is concerned, and a remarkable number of notable histrions delighted London playgoers.

The patronage which the Court[1] extended to theatrical displays (Plate 49)—a tradition carried on since the time of Charles II—was responsible for much in making the theatre an objective to many who under less auspicious circumstances might have been obliged to direct their talent into uncongenial channels. The number of play-houses was comparatively few, but was adequate to the then relatively small population of London; and there was an intelligent and quite special interest taken in the performances, which were probably the better appreciated, because they were far fewer in number than in our own days. More was thought of the play and less of its setting, and Shakespeare was popular because of the beauty of the "book" rather than because of the elaboration of the *mise en scène*. Great writers like Lamb and Hazlitt criticised the performances of great actors like Liston, Elliston, Kean, Kemble and Munden, and even the destruction by fire of Covent Garden was responsible for one of the most successful *jeu d'esprits* in the language.[2]

As one looks through contemporary records one is dazzled by the illustrious names that figured on the play-bills. Mrs. Siddons, whose most signal triumphs are associated with this period, died in 1831; her brother, J. P. Kemble, acted till the end in 1823; Elliston, after his Drury Lane failure, was at the Olympic, where Madame Vestris first appeared, before going to the Lyceum in 1847. Tom Dibden delighted the habitués of the Surrey Theatre (which he considered the best in London or the suburbs) from 1816 to 1822; G. F. Cooke acted at the Royalty in Well-close Square, and thought, not unnaturally, when he got there that he had arrived at the end of the world. Miss Stephens, afterwards Lady Essex, first appeared at the Pantheon in those early days, and Grimaldi kept London screaming with laughter at Sadler's Wells, any time between 1812 and 1828. Bannister made his last bow to the public in 1815, and, perhaps the most notable of all—the incomparable Edmund Kean, died, after astonishing his contemporaries,

---

[1] On the arrival of the Sovereign at a theatre, it was customary, down to the time of Victoria, for the manager to meet the Royal party at the entrance, and with a candle in each hand to light them to the royal box (Plate 49).

[2] The O.P. (Old Prices) riots of 1809 show not only the interest taken in the theatre, but the uncompromising attitude of the public towards any innovation in its management.

in 1833, to be followed by his son, Charles, nothing like so good an actor as his father, but a stage manager of the first rank, who was prominent in the rather arid theatrical period that immediately succeeded this great one, till his death in 1868. At an earlier date, the short but effulgent appearance of Master Betty—"the Infant Roscius," showed how good judges could be taken off their guard, and could suppose that youthful promise was an earnest of matured success.[1]

During the earlier years of Queen Victoria's reign the Haymarket Theatre was a focus for all kinds of talent under the management of Benjamin Webster. There Charles Matthews, the younger, played "Sir Charles Coldstream," one of the most finished performances of that or any time, according to all accounts; there appeared Macready, at a salary of £4,000 a season; there Charles Kean acted, after his unfortunate speculation at Covent Garden; and there, to take but a few names from a long and illustrious roll, might have been seen Samuel Phelps and Madame Celeste; Mrs. Stirling (who linked up those early days with our own), and Buckstone, a favourite with Queen Victoria, and the hero of a hundred anecdotes.

Some illustrations which are here reproduced (Plates 48 & 49) will give an idea of the appearance of the interior of a theatre during the period. The prominence and space accorded to the pit will be remarked, and supplies point to the saying that that portion of the house was the best from which to see the play. The lack of comfort in the seating will also be noticed, as will a variety of other features helping to differentiate the play-house of that period from the luxurious lounge it has since become.[2]

[1] He made his first appearance in London, at Covent Garden, on Dec. 1st., 1804, when the crush was indescribable; see Doran's "Annals of the Stage."

[2] It is interesting to remember that Patent Theatres were abolished by Act of Parliament in 1843.

CHAPTER VI.

FUN AND FROLIC

WE are traditionally supposed to take our pleasures sadly, at least this is the conclusion come to by our friends across the Channel. Like all generalizations, however, the dictum can hardly be said to be fundamentally sound. As a matter of fact, we take our pleasures in a more or less boisterous and full-blooded way; and during the earlier years of the 19th century this was even more the case. It was the period when the recreations of the people did not confine themselves to silent attention to anything. If it was a bull-fight, or a bear-fight,[1] a cock-fight or a prize-fight, or a hotly contested election, each of these shows drew an audience which was as vociferous as it was large; and the noise and excitement to-day associated with the classic event on Epsom Heath, were then in evidence at all sorts of places where strength was pitted against strength, or where muscle and sinew were alone helpless against science and technique.

During the first half of the 19th century pugilism was rampant in this country. It was the favourite amusement among all classes in practically every county, each of which possessed its particular prize-fighters patronised by the gentry and regarded with a sort of wondering admiration by the lower classes. A contemporary authority says " Magistrates then took very little trouble to hunt the Gullys and Tom Sprigs from Surrey into Berkshire and from Berkshire into Buckinghamshire. They somewhat too frequently had their rendezvous within a dozen miles of Windsor. The only exhibition of pugilism I ever saw was perfectly unmolested by justice or constable. It was on Maidenhead Thicket, where the renowned Pierce Egan, with a considerate regard for a brother of the Press, got me a good place out of which I escaped as fast as ever I could when I saw young Dutch Sam fall across the ropes with a broken arm."[2] The fact is the sport had taken so great a hold on

[1] In 1802 an attempt was made by Parliament to put a stop to both these amusements with which Hockley was identified, but in spite of the protests of Sheridan and Wilberforce, they had a legal status till 1835, when they were suppressed.

[2] Knight.

the people that in spite of laws and regulations, little interference was made with prize-fights, and although these often took place in localities and at times, ostensibly selected in order to evade notice, the crowd that duly assembled with impunity to witness the combats, whether it was one between John Gully and Robert Gregson, the Lancashire giant, or between Cribb and Nichol, or Belcher and Mendoza, or Gentleman Jackson (the friend and tutor of Byron, who gave lessons at his rooms at 13, Bond Street) and "The Game Chicken," proved that the Law discreetly kept its eyes closed and refrained from exercising its power at the risk of a riot (Plate 50).[1]

Although such encounters naturally had their *venue* outside cities and towns, they often took place so close to these centres that a drive enabled the spectators to be present at them, and a Frenchman who visited England in 1810, records witnessing one of these encounters, in this case between the negro Molyneux and Rimmer, a Lancashire pugilist, at Molesey Hurst, about 15 miles from London. "The battle," he says, "lasted half an hour—about twenty rounds—the Lancashire man always thrown; when all at once the barrier was broken—an irruption of the mob took place and soon became general, rushing towards the centre and overwhelming the ring and its occupants—hats flew; cries rent the air;

the black, meantime, grinning over his fallen adversary. There were no ragged coats in sight, and *half the mob were gentlemen.*"

[1] Mendoza was the first to go on tour, and to hold sparring matches which did much towards bringing the use of gloves into fashion.
In 1814 boxing with gloves had become so fashionable that the Allied Sovereigns were given an exhibition of the art at Lord Lowther's in Pall Mall, and also at Angelo's fencing rooms in St. James's Street.

"The Interior of the Fives Court"
A Sparring Match in Progress between Randall and Turner
By T. Blake

PLATE 52

THE LAST STEEPLECHASE AT THE HIPPODROME RACECOURSE, KENSINGTON (1841)

By H. Alken

THE BETTING RING AT EPSOM (1836)

By James Pollard

PLATE 53

A Skit on the Hobbyhorse Craze: "Going to the Races" (1819)

The Hobbyhorse School (circa 1820)

From Contemporary Prints

Ascot Races

From a Contemporary Print

PLATE 54

FUN AND FROLIC

This last piece of information is not surprising. We know that such men as William Windham and Dr. Parr were strong advocates of the prize ring; and it is recorded of the Lord Spencer of the period that once, at Wiseton Hall, his seat near East Retford, a discussion at dinner arising concerning a recent case of stabbing, he held forth at length on the advantages of prize-fighting and boxing as being likely to obviate the un-English practise of using the knife; and he became so eloquent that his biographer says it was the only occasion that he heard him speak with eagerness and almost with passion.

Some of the London centres of prize-fighting and boxing may be mentioned. One was the Fives Court, in St. Martin's Street, which was a very favourite resort (Plate 51). Then there was Daffy's Club, held at Tom Belcher's at the Castle Tavern, Holborn, a place recorded in "The London Spy"; and the Pugilistic Society, mentioned by Byron, which held its first meeting at the Thatched House Tavern, on May 22nd, 1814; while such exponents as Gregson and Gully, Broughton and Slack were wont to foregather at Limmer's Hotel and there meet their patrons and pupils. The importance of the prize-fighters once received a royal *imprimatur*. For when George IV feared trouble at his Coronation owing to his lack of popularity with the mob, in consequence of his treatment of Queen Caroline, he arranged to have a body-guard headed by Jackson—"the Emperor of Pugilism"— the members of which were clothed in scarlet and gold liveries and duly kept order on the eventful day.[1]

Dog-fighting, cock-fighting (Plate 40) and pigeon-shooting, were other forms of amusement in which all classes, whether as protagonists or spectators, took part. There was, as we have seen, a cock-pit in the cellars of Crockford's, and there were other centres for this so-called sport in various parts of the Town, survivals from the 18th. century still continuing in vogue during the earlier years of the following century. But it was chiefly in country places that cock-fighting was most popular. Much the same may be said with regard to dog-fights, which were publicly advertised, and received patronage from "the nobility and gentry of these realms." Many of these forms of recreation were, of course, but mediums for betting, and in the case of dog-fighting enormous sums were paid for famous combatants, and bets running often into thousands, were laid on

---

[1] See Miles's "Pugilistica" and other similar sources, for details of the Ring during this period.

the results of such encounters. The fact is, the full-blooded life of the preceding century was dying hard, and it was perhaps as much owing to the effeminacy introduced by the dandies, that such things gradually went into abeyance, at least among the upper classes, as to the gradual development of less strenuous characteristics, and the softening of manners brought about by a larger and more dignified conception of life, which advancing years brought in their train.

Another form of amusement was the Turf. At Newmarket and Doncaster, and elsewhere in the country, the great race meetings were strongly patronised; while Ascot (Plate 54), always an essentially Royal meeting owing to the proximity of the Castle, and the official recognition given it by the presence of Royalty and the Master of the Buckhounds, and still more Epsom (Plate 52), due to its closeness to London, drew crowds which became denser year by year.

The Derby (Plate 41) has always taken the lead in the annals of racing, ever since those classic stakes had been started by the twelfth Earl of that name in 1780 (he had initiated the Oaks in the preceding year); and the interest taken in racing by George, Prince of Wales, from 1800 to 1807 in which year, owing to the trouble arising from the riding of his jockey, Sam Chiffney, he gave up the Turf in disgust—imparted a special impetus to the sport which has continued to be the most characteristic of the English speaking race; the one in which it shows to the best advantage, and, in spite of all the questionable features associated with it, the one in which great traditions still survive. What a hold racing had by then taken on the minds of the upper classes is indicated in the pages of Charles Greville's diary, where details concerning it are set forth with the same meticulous care as are the inner workings of cabinets or the *vie intime* of illustrious personages. Greville looked after the training stable of the Duke of York, and might, therefore, be expected to take a particular interest in this direction; but he was symptomatic of his period—a period when men of affairs unbent themselves at Epsom or Ascot, and took as much interest in horse-flesh, as the men of leisure who regarded it as a *délassement* from the monotony of a merely decorative existence.

During one part of our period there was a race-course actually in London. It was known as the Hippodrome and was situated where Ladbrooke Square and its adjoining streets are now (Plate 52).

FUN AND FROLIC

The principal entrance was opposite the present Notting Hill Gate Railway Station, and the eminence on which St. John's Church stands was close by within its boundaries. From a contemporary description it would appear to have flourished as a racecourse from 1837 to 1841, and it was not long before the residents in the neighbourhood signed a petition to prevent racing on Sundays, which seems to have been successful. By 1844 all trace of the racecourse had become obliterated, and nothing but open ground remained in its place. The inhabitants had insisted on a right of way across the area, and having taken the law into their own hands, had removed, with the aid of saws and hatchets, the various barriers, thus causing the racing fraternity to abandon it. A contemporary picture shows the racecourse, with its stand and booths, running round the rising ground; and H. Alken, junior, made a set of four aquatints, reproduced by C. Hunt, entitled " The Last Grand Steeplechase at the Hippodrome Racecourse," which possess a countrified air very difficult to associate with the present thickly covered area as we now know it.

To-day Football and Cricket are the chief forms of amusement of the general Londoner. It is, however, a rather curious fact that during the first half of the 19th century, the popularity of the former game was in abeyance. This is the more remarkable because it is an ancient game, and even so early as the reign of Edward II, an act was passed forbidding the populace " to hustle over large balls " in the streets of London, on account of the evils likely to arise from the practise; while in the time of Edward III, the game is expressly termed " football"—the earliest mention of the name, by the bye. The fact, however, remains that not till the starting of the famous Blackheath Club in 1859, followed by that of Richmond in the next year, did football really begin that recrudescence of popularity which has attached to it ever since and which, to-day, makes it (at least according to the contents bills of the evening papers) more important than changes of ministries or the declarations of war.

With cricket it was otherwise. The Hambledon Club flourished from 1750 to 1791. But before its institution there the game had been played, for it had become, we are told, the subject of wagers, and an act, 9 Anne c. 19, sought to put it down, although the Court of Queen's Bench decided in its favour, and it is known to have flourished at Bromley, in Kent, before being played in Hampshire. Even till the first few years of the 19th century heavy wagers were laid, and matches played for very high stakes. In 1787 the M.C.C. was inaugurated, and from that time forward London may properly be regarded as the official headquarters of the game. The annals of Lords and the M.C.C. have been compiled by Lord Harris and F. A. Ashley-Cooper, Esq., and therein may be read the accounts of those Homeric contests on the three grounds which Thomas Lord successively took, the last of these being the present one, whose history dates from 1813, the year in which Lord obtained possession of it. It was not till thirty odd years later that the first sod was laid of the present Oval, a circumstance which converted what had been a vast market garden into something rivalling Lords, and from the point of view of the bulk of London's cricket lovers, a more popular rival. In old maps (Mogg's, dated 1808, for instance) the Oval will be found marked; but it was not then used as a cricket ground, although its early name has in consequence become associated with the most patronised centre of the game.

Malcolm, recording the recreations of the Londoner of 1807, thus sums up those pleasures in which the upper classes indulged during the earlier years of the century. Says he, " The amusements of the rich and noble consists of every possible enjoyment: birthdays, levées, breakfasts at *private* houses attended by two or three hundred persons at three or four o'clock in the afternoon, dinners, card-parties, suppers and *routs*—other amusements of the great consist in riding through Hyde Park; the ladies in their coaches, and the gentlemen on horse-back in an adjoining road (Plate 37). He that would judge of the population of London should attend in the Park on any Sunday at three o'clock, from February till May: he must be astonished at the sight. The coaches, the horses, the populace of every rank who toil against the bleak east winds, are wonderfully numerous. Nor should he omit a visit to Kensington Gardens in May, to view the beautiful pedestrians that form our fashionable world; or a winter excursion to the Serpentine river and the canal in St. James's Park, where numbers skate or attempt to skate." "It would," he concludes, "be useless to more than mention the additional pursuits of the rich, who visit the annual exhibitions of Paintings and other attractive objects with eagerness, the Playhouse, Vauxhall, etc., etc., but alas! London becomes a mere blank after the 4th of June. *Nobody* remains in *Town*; it is too hot, too suffocating. *Everybody* therefore retires to their seats, *if they have them*; and the rest fly to

A Charity Bazaar in Spring Gardens (1832)

By G. Scharf

Peace Celebrations: The Model Fleet at Anchor on the Serpentine (1814)

From a Contemporary Print

AFTER THE ELECTION: THE WINNING CANDIDATE'S PROGRESS THROUGH HIS CONSTITUENCY (1808)
From a Contemporary Print

PLATE 56

PLATE 57

A Punch and Judy Show (1821)

By J. A. Atkinson

The Chimney Sweep (1821)

By J. A. Atkinson

PLATE 58

OLD COVENT GARDEN MARKET
From a Drawing by G. Scharf

THE OPENING OF NEW HUNGERFORD MARKET
From a Contemporary Print

FUN AND FROLIC

Margate, Ramsgate, and Brighton, those *capacious* receptacles. Such are the follies of many."

The doings of Jerry and Corinthian Tom may be somewhat highly coloured by the pen of Pierce Egan, as they are by the pencil of the Cruikshanks, but there is no doubt that their excursions into all sorts of low haunts, their predilection for "blue ruin," their mania for over-turning Charlies in their boxes, or for foregathering with thieves and cadgers in the back slums of the "Holy Land," with the inevitable frequent appearances at Bow Street, and their sojourns in spongeing houses,[1] represent with some exaggeration, the habits of many a young blood of the period and often of men of position who were of an age to know very much better (Plates 11, 11a, 27, 38 & 40). Indeed, the Mohocks of the preceding century had their successors in those Regency Bucks who could be, and often were, decorative and dandiacal in the West, but whose chief delight was to be vulgar and noisy in the East. A short life and a merry one was their motto, and they lived up (or shall we say down) to it, with a vengeance (Plate 20).

But, after all, such doings represented but the life of a relatively small section of society. The working classes (tradespeople and artisans and so forth) were kept busy during the day, and were often too tired out at night to do anything but sleep. Some of them went to the play, many frequented the public-houses where clubs and harmonious meetings catered for their recreation. But as a rule what freedom they obtained from work was only to be enjoyed on a Sunday when the shops were shut, and the citizen and his family of all classes, were wont to frequent those "Wells" and Tea Gardens, and other places of amusement, many of which were survivors of the 18th century; although these were not nearly so numerous as they had formerly been.

By George Cruikshank.

For instance, such places as Marylebone Gardens; Spa Fields;

---

[1] The spongeing houses of the period were to be found in many quarters; one in Chancery Lane is familiar to us as being the place where Titmarsh was shut up and Rawdon Crawley.

LIFE IN REGENCY AND EARLY VICTORIAN TIMES

The London Spa; the New Wells, near by; the Mulberry Garden, Clerkenwell; Belvedere House and Gardens, Lambeth; The Flora Tea Gardens, Waterloo Bridge Road; and the Dog and Duck, in St. George's Fields, had all practically disappeared with the new century, or only overlapped it for so short a time as to be negligible in the history of contemporary manners. But many remained and, in spite of having lost much of their original character, were yet carried on with profit to their owners and recreation to the Londoner whose position in society did not permit of his enjoying anything better.

Islington Spa, for instance, which had once enjoyed a great vogue, was beginning to lose its attractions at the commencement of the 19th century, although Malcolm, in 1803, speaks of its gardens as still being " really very beautiful." Alterations were made here in 1810, and in 1825 a new proprietor opened the place as a "Spa;" but 1840 saw the end of it, and Spa Cottages were built on the site of what had once been an important feature in London's recreations.

Sadler's Wells, in consequence of its theatre, enjoyed still a successful career, largely because it continually altered its attractions and catered for all sorts of changing tastes. Pony races were a feature here in 1802, and four years later a regular racecourse was laid out. In 1803 Belzoni, of exploration fame, exhibited here his feats of strength; later Mrs. Graham made from the grounds her sensational balloon ascents, and here Grimaldi secured some of his greatest triumphs from 1819 to 1828; while Samuel Phelps, who had become proprietor in 1844, gave his series of Shakespeare's plays in the theatre, where in 1832 T. P. Cooke had made his first appearance as William in " Black-eyed Susan." During the early years of the century the rural characteristics of the place are thus recorded by John Britton: "At the end of the last century and beginning of the present," he says, " Sadler's Wells was truly a suburban theatre—being surrounded by fields. . . . There were not any public lamps, and men and boys with flambeaus were in attendance on dark nights to light persons across the fields to the nearest streets of Islington, Clerkenwell and Gray's Inn Lane "!

Another once popular haunt that survived, but had lost much of its original character, was *Bagnigge Wells*, which by 1810 had become a very low-class resort indeed. In 1813 it was put up for sale, and in the following year was re-opened by one Stock.

FUN AND FROLIC

Success was not however achieved by the new proprietor, and after many changes of hands the place was closed in 1841.

Indeed, it will be found that such haunts as survived the beginning of the century generally came to grief about the middle of it. *The Peerless Pool* was one of these; and although it possessed a different character from others here mentioned, being really a sort of elaborate bathing establishment, it may be included in this list, because it was reconstructed by Joseph Watts in 1805, and certainly justified its existence—if only because it gave pleasure to many a young Blue-Coat Boy—down to 1850.

In the Picture of London for 1823 the *Bayswater Tea Gardens* are given as among those frequented by the middle classes. From 1836 onwards the name was changed to the *Flora Tea Gardens*, and in that year Mrs. Graham (whom we have already met with elsewhere) made a balloon ascent here; as did another well-known aeronaut, named Hampton, three years later; the latter descending in a parachute, not without danger. Subsequently the place was renamed the *Victoria Tea Gardens*, where running matches and such like athletic attractions had a vogue till about 1854, when the gardens were abolished and the houses of Lancaster Gate built on their site.

Another resort of a somewhat similar character was the *White Conduit House* whose surroundings at the beginning of the century were quite rural, but whose amenities after a lapse of thirty odd years were largely spoilt by the rows of houses that had sprung up in the neighbourhood. Cloudesley Place and Albert Street mark approximately the situation of the White Conduit House, and anyone acquainted with that now thickly populated area will realise from the fact of these tea gardens having been among fields and lanes at the beginning of the 19th century, what an extraordinary building development has taken place here since that date.

From 1811, or earlier, till 1828, the White Conduit House was a favourite resort of the citizens, who came here to dance and drink tea. Balloon ascents and fireworks (a form of amusement that gradually took a great hold on popular imagination) varied the more sober recreations; and so successful was the place that in 1825 it was called the new Vauxhall. It continued its activities till 1849, when it was closed; the gradual enveloping movement of new buildings having taken from it that rural character on which it largely relied for public favour.

LIFE IN REGENCY AND EARLY VICTORIAN TIMES

Such places as *Copenhagen House*, a very favourite Sunday resort from 1816 to 1830, which finally came to an end in 1852 when the Corporation bought the property and began the erection of the Metropolitan Cattle Market; *Highbury Barn* (a kind of North London Cremorne), another Sunday resort, which existed, although towards the end somewhat precariously, till the 'seventies; and *Hornsey Wood House* may be thus alluded to as centres where the middle classes fore-gathered in those portions of London where, to-day, a tea-garden would be sadly out of place. In other parts of the metropolis certain survivals might have been met with, such as *St. Helena Gardens*, Rotherhithe, notable for its fireworks and concerts, even so late as the 'eighties; the *Cumberland Tea Gardens*, at Vauxhall, much frequented by South Londoners during the first quarter of the 19th century; *Cromwell's Tea Gardens*, adjoining Hale House, Kensington, a little east of Gloucester Road, known later as the *Florida Tea Gardens;* and *Cuper's Gardens*, cut up in 1814, when Waterloo Bridge and its approaches were constructed.

Of the two chief places of amusement of this sort, famous during the 18th century, *Ranelagh* and *Vauxhall*, the fates were very different. The former only just survived the opening of the new century, and with the ball given there by Boodle's Club in 1802, when the ladies wore, we are told, "white and silver ornamented with laurels"; and the ball, in the following year, commemorating the Installation of the Knights of the Bath, its glories came to an end, it being opened for the last time on July 8th, 1803.

Vauxhall, on the other hand, continued with undiminished popularity till 1859. Its firework displays, its vocal concerts, at which such performers as Darley, Mrs. Franklin, Mrs. Mountain, Charles Dignum, and Mrs. Bland, were protagonists; its tight-rope audacities, in the person of Madame Saqui, of Paris; its "20,000 additional lamps"; its rack-punch, its jugglers—Ramo Samee, for instance; its later singers, Braham, whom Lamb so loved, Miss Stephens, who became a Countess, and Madame Vestris whose singing of "Cherry Ripe" caused a mild sensation; all these things, together with Ducrow and his wonderful horsemanship, and the ubiquitous Simpson—master of the ceremonies and head and front of the undertaking for so many years, whose benefit in 1833 was a kind of triumph recorded by pen and pencil in the daily press, made Vauxhall not only popular but famous; so that it is perhaps the only resort of this kind that bulks as largely in the social history

FUN AND FROLIC

of the first half of the 19th century, as it did in the last half of the 18th.

The works of Dickens and Thackeray are full of references to the place which Cruikshank and Doyle have recorded in another medium; and in "Vanity Fair" and the "Sketches by Boz," as well as in the Bird's Eye-View of Society, we have pictures of that haunt of pleasure which comes down to us after many years as a place with an immense band-stand and innumerable lamps—a sort of Whistler effect tempered by the slim waists of one pictorial satirist and the ample crinolines of the other.[1]

It ought not to require the name of Whistler to remind us of yet another centre of pleasure which enjoyed great popularity during a later period—I mean *Cremorne*; but it does. That wonderful "Nocturne" which aroused the ire of Ruskin and gave rise to a *cause célèbre*, is what the present generation will think of when Cremorne is mentioned. The place comes within our purview, for it flourished from 1843 onwards, being closed in 1877, and during that period it became a sort of Vauxhall—indeed, many of the pictures that adorned the older establishment found their way to the Banquetting Hall of its younger rival. Cremorne (Plate 59), may be said to have been rather notorious than famous. It was a sort of commonplace copy of its prototype, and it came to an end in consequence of complaints made by the inhabitants of the vicinity (it was just west of Battersea Bridge, on the river) who were disturbed by the noise and licence which obtained there.

But it bulked largely among centres of amusement during our period, and for that reason deserves to be remembered. It was named after Viscount Cremorne who became possessed of the property in 1803. Twenty odd years later (to be precise, in 1825) it was purchased by Mr. Granville Penn, and from him passed to "Anastasius" Hope. The gardens were originally opened to the public under the name of the Stadium, but did not at first prove a success. With a new management however, and a changed name—Cremorne Gardens—it became very popular, and its twelve acres are enthusiastically described by a contemporary as "a Vale of Tempe"! All sorts of amusements were provided—concerts, ballets, *tableaux vivants*, equestrian feats, and fireworks; and its river frontage gave it an additional attraction. Indeed,

[1] Tom Moore records going there on a wet night, and speaks of the dreary effect; "worse than the desert of Arabia," as Hughes the proprietor remarked.

its name survives as a sort of successor, on a much less ambitious scale, and catering for a different class of people, to that of Ranelagh, —a Ranelagh of a more prosaic and less decorative period.

Rosherville Gardens was another place of not dissimilar character, (established in 1837); but in its far off fastness at Gravesend, it could only be regarded as appealing, as a rule, to a more or less local population. At the same time, being on the river, and thus within easy reach by the steam-boats, which then formed the means of many a pleasant jaunt for Londoners, it maintained a sort of aquatic connection with the centre of the Metropolis. Rosherville itself was constructed by a Mr. Jeremiah Rosher, hence the name, and Gaspey speaks of it as "a kind of Cheltenham in miniature, with its extensive gardens to stroll through, the Arcadian groves for which no inconsiderable number of our social companions leave the steamboat." "On Gala-nights," he adds, " fireworks wind up the amusements of Rosherville Gardens, where certainly every expedient is resorted to to drive dull care away." Among the attractions were a maze, a bear-pit, a monkey-cavern; while " birds of tropical plumage " were to be seen flying about, and the visitor seeking refreshment, found it in what was grandiloquently styled " The Baronial Hall."

Yet another place of resort was the *Eagle Tavern and Gardens*, which succeeded the Old Shepherd and Shepherdess, in the City Road, and was built about 1825 (it was reconstructed in 1838). It was, with its theatre and Grecian saloon, its gardens and its dancing-room, quite a famous place of amusement, and continued to be well into the century; nearly until 1882, in fact, when it was purchased by General Booth for the headquarters of the Salvation Army.[1]

The River was a considerable source of amusement to the Londoner of the period, although as a means of social transit (so

---

[1] One ought to mention the famous Chelsea Bun House, which had been spoken of by Swift (Journal to Stella, 1712), and which continued to be patronised by visitors to Ranelagh. It is said that on Good Friday, April 18th, 1839, no fewer than 240,000 buns were sold here. Soon after, however, the place was pulled down and sold, together with all its quaint contents dating from an earlier day.

I may remind the reader that the once well-known Red House, at Battersea, was a rendezvous for pigeon shooting, " an establishment," according to a contemporary writer, " expressly intended for the lovers of the sport." Sport, forsooth!

(See picture in " The Mirror," for April 6th, 1839).

FUN AND FROLIC

to term it) its heyday passed with the 18th century. The coming of the steamboat, however, gave it an importance from the point of view of a pleasure resort, which more than equalled, although not so decoratively, its earlier importance in this respect (Plate 60). The first steamboat went to Richmond in 1814; in the following year Gravesend was linked up, in this way, with the Metropolis; and a few months later excursions were even begun to Margate—the Margate steamers superseding the old sailing "hoys." Steam traffic increased by leaps and bounds, until a few years after the middle of the century no fewer than three million people are said annually to have landed and embarked at the "Old Shades" pier; numbers, however, which the extension of the railway system greatly reduced as time went on.

The Folly on the Thames, which had attracted so many at an earlier day, had disappeared, but a Chinese Junk was moored on its site (nearly opposite Somerset House) in 1848, and was visited by thousands—Dickens, who has left an account of it, among them—who on other occasions flocked to the Thames, frozen over in 1811, and in 1814 when that great "Frost Fair" was held (rivalling the earlier one of 1683), which was heralded by a fog of such magnitude as to cause even the usually sedate Hughson to speak of it with excitement.

As Grosley once confidently asserted that the height of the parapets of the London bridges was due to an attempt on the part of the authorities to lessen the number of suicides (!), one may, I suppose, include a word or two on these structures as having some bearing, if not on the fun and frolic, at least on the follies of a period succeeding that in which the Frenchman visited our shores.

During the first half of the 19th century, London possessed eight bridges. By Mogg's plan, dated 1808, we find but three marked, those of London, Blackfriars and Westminster. Old London Bridge was rebuilt in the twenties and was opened, in great state, by William IV on August 1st, 1831. Old Westminster Bridge, on which Wordsworth, in 1803, wrote his famous sonnet, remained till 1859, when the new one, rather lower down the river was commenced; and Blackfriars Bridge, which Mylne had begun in 1760, also lasted past the middle of the 19th century. Of those that came into existence between 1800 and 1850, Vauxhall Bridge was opened in 1816; Waterloo Bridge, which was originally to have been called Wellington Bridge, with great military display, by the Prince Regent, on June 18th, 1817; Southwark Bridge, at midnight, on March 24th, 1879; Hammersmith Suspension Bridge in 1827; and Vauxhall Bridge on June 4th, 1816. In addition Old Battersea Bridge (not shown in early 19th century plans of London, as being outside the area !) remained; the wooden structure which had been erected by Holland in 1771-2, only being closed in 1881 as unsafe.

The fact that in the early years of the 19th century only three bridges existed in the then restricted area of London, caused much traffic to be carried on by the watermen who plied their boats up and down the stream and between different points on the two shores of the river; and thus helped for a time to carry on that 18th century tradition when the Thames was not only a highway for commerce but also for pleasure.

The annual fairs held in different parts of the Metropolis afforded other outlets for popular exuberance. Although the heyday of such institutions, so far as London is concerned, passed with the preceding century, certain of them survived, but often enough in a modified, and, from what they had once been, an almost unrecognisable, form. The fairs once held at Southwark, Parson's Green, Kennington Common, and Brook Green, had ceased to exist by the beginning of the 19th century; others, such as those of Camberwell, Battersea, Clapham Common and Blackheath, carried on a sort of precarious existence till past the middle of the period; that at Peckham, having become a nuisance, was abolished, in 1827. Wandsworth, too (where in 1826 an attempt was made to revive the once famous election of the Mayor of Garratt,[1] an attempt that failed) once had its Fair, and some of its theatrical and other attractions are recorded so late as 1840. The better known Mayfair had ceased to exist, although it had survived to within a few years of the 19th century; but the ancient Edmonton Fair was still a living thing in 1820, and among its attractions are recorded some daring feats of a lion tamer—anticipating Van Amburgh, who, by the bye, gave thrills to many a Londoner during the earlier half of our period, and provided one of those subsidiary shows which were then as the sands of the sea.

But the chief of the London Fairs during the first half of the century were those of Bartholomew and Greenwich. The former, whose rowdyness has been recorded by the boisterous audacities

[1] See Hone's "Every Day Book."

THE ENTRANCE TO CREMORNE

THE ROYAL MARIONETTE THEATRE IN CREMORNE GARDENS
From Contemporary Drawings

Embarking in Pleasure-Steamers near Southwark Bridge (1841)

By W. Parrott

PLATE 60

FUN AND FROLIC

of Rowlandson, was, however, on the wane. In 1801 it was crowded with pickpockets; in the following year " Lady Holland's Mob,"[1] as it used to be called, made itself a terror to law-abiding citizens who ventured into its vicinity. But still the meeting was permitted to go on, in spite of complaints and protests. Richardson's shows continued, and the " learned pig " attracted the credulous. Hone, writing in 1825, has left an account of the place, with its " Living Skeleton," its Wombwell's wonderful elephant, its noise, and its dubious habitués. Gradually it became shorn of those features which had attracted generations of Londoners, and although it lingered on till 1850 it had, to quote one authority, sunk down to a few gilt ginger-bread stalls.

Greenwich Fairs (for there were two) were held annually at Easter and Whitsun. In the "Calender of Amusements" (Albert Smith) for 1840, there is a long and circumstantial account of them, wherein they are grandiloquently termed "great national events"!— and Planché, twenty years earlier, thought them worthy of description in his " Recollections." But even greater men have recorded their experiences at these places, and from the pens of Thackeray and Dickens we have word pictures of the fairs—word pictures which require no repetition here, as most of my readers will know them for themselves.[2] Indeed, in the pages of the two great novelists one can get a better idea of certain phases of London life during the second quarter of the 19th century, than can be obtained from volumes written in the dry-as-dust manner so beloved of earlier topographers. In their novels and shorter tales and sketches, the life of the people is unrolled before us by the hands of these two magicians; and it is probable that with their aid, supplemented by the illustrative art of Cruikshank, Doyle, and Leech, we shall obtain a truer conception of the period from 1837 to 1850, so far as domestic life is concerned, than from any other source whatever.

It is obviously impossible, in a rapid survey, to particularise all the various centres of recreation and amusement, which were open to the London public at this period. Bullock's museum in Piccadilly, opened in 1812 by Mr. Bullock of Liverpool, which cost £30,000, and was closed as a museum in 1819, is one

[1] No one seems to know the origin of this phrase.
[2] See Thackeray's " Sketches and Travels in London," and Dickens's " Sketches by Boz."

LIFE IN REGENCY AND EARLY VICTORIAN TIMES

that should be mentioned, however, because as the Egyptian Hall it has been familiar to most of us, although its site knows it no more. Here, after the dispersal of Bullock's collection, all sorts of shows took place. Here, Géricault exhibited his famous " Wreck of the Medusa," in 1820 ; here, a model of the Egyptian Sarcophagus, the original of which is now in the Soane Museum, was exhibited, in the following year ; here, a collection of curiosities from Mexico and Central America were on view in 1824 ; and here, *inter multa alia*, the Siamese Twins were to be seen in 1829 ; and in 1846 " General " Tom Thumb here drew vast crowds, to the disgust of poor Haydon, whose pictures, exhibited in another part of the building, hardly attracted anyone.

In addition to such " indoor " amusements, of which the Egyptian Hall must serve as the solitary specimen,[1] there were the two Zoological Gardens which vied with each other for popularity. That in Regent's Park requires only a word, because it is, in its greatly enlarged form, known to everyone. It was first opened in 1828,[2] the principal founders being Sir Humphrey Davy and Sir Stamford Raffles. It had its origin in the formation of the Royal Zoological Society which had been instituted in 1826, and incorporated by Royal charter three years later.

The other somewhat similar establishment was known as the Surrey Zoological Gardens, and was situated in Panton Place, Kennington. It contained the menagerie collected by Mr. Cross who laid out the place in 1831-2. The grounds covered about 15 acres and comprised a lake of nearly 3 acres. The collection of animals was a very complete one, and a contemporary writer says that the carnivoræ " were contained in a curvilinear glazed building 300 feet in diameter." These gardens were differentiated from their more scientific rivals on the other bank, by offering such attractions as nightly fêtes where Jullien's famed orchestra performed, and panoramic spectacles, such as representations of Vesuvius, the siege of Gibraltar, Napoleon crossing the Alps, etc.

---

[1] It was a great age for panoramas of all sorts, and the Cosmorama, in Regent Street ; the Cyclorama in Albany Street ; the Diorama, in the Regent's Park ; Burford's Panorama, in Leicester Square ; and Banvard's, at the Egyptian Hall, may be mentioned as the chief of such forms of amusement. Madame Tussaud's also opened first at the Lyceum in 1802, and continued increasing in size and popularity till its final destruction by fire lately.

[2] What appears to have been the first illustrated guide to the gardens was published just ten years later.

The Coronation of George IV in Westminster Abbey

From the Painting by P. Stephanoff

PLATE 62

The King's Herb-Woman with her six Maids

The Duke of Wellington as High Constable of England

The Duke of York in his Royal Robes

THE CORONATION OF GEORGE IV

From Paintings by P. Stephanoff

FUN AND FROLIC

The price of admission was a shilling, and in 1837 fireworks (with what effect on the animals report sayeth not) were introduced. On a part of the grounds the Surrey Music Hall was subsequently erected, where Thackeray once gave some of his readings. This building was destroyed by fire in 1861 and the gardens were closed in 1877, houses being erected on their site and Panton Street and Manor Place approximately marking their former boundaries.

One other centre of amusement claims a word or two—the Argyll Rooms. They stood on the east side of Regent Street, at the corner of Little Argyll Street, and were built by Nash in 1818. Here balls and masquerades were held; here the Philharmonic Society gave its concerts till 1830, concerts at which such men as Spohr, Weber and Mendelssohn, appeared at various times; here Chabert—the once well-remembered "Fire King"—gave his astonishing exhibitions. The rooms were burnt down in 1830. They are not to be confounded with the later Argyll Rooms of rather unsavoury memory, which stood where the Trocadero is now.

During the period under consideration, apart from the recognised forms of amusement and recreation which obtained, such as those I have already touched upon in this chapter, various events occurred which were in the character of nine days' wonders, but which afforded the Londoner of the time opportunities for outings or, in the case of the idle, means of escape from the boredom and monotony of existence.

Among such things the three coronations, those of George IV, William IV, and Victoria, should be mentioned. The first was, up to that time, the most magnificent that had ever taken place (Plates 61 & 62). George IV was nothing if not decorative. He was the dandy of kings, and the trouble and expense incurred in making his coronation a thing to be remembered, were appropriate to his character. It happened, however, that owing to his treatment of his wife he was exceedingly unpopular at the time. Even the Dandies, as a body, were hostile; and so anxious was he to secure their suffrages that a magnificent breakfast was prepared for them at Westminster, and the timely attention had the effect of satisfactorily overcoming their antagonism. But the coronation was not to pass off without its *contretemps*; for Caroline of Brunswick was advised to press her right of admission to the Abbey, and the unique sight was presented to Londoners of a rightful queen-consort knockingly vainly at the doors of the edifice in which her husband was being officially proclaimed head of the State.

The coronation of William IV, ten years later, was not attended by any trouble; but at the same time, as a show, it fell far short of what had preceded it. That of George IV had cost no less than £240,000; and it was determined that William's should be cheaper and simpler. One of the reasons for this was the fear of revolution entertained by many influential people. However, everything went off well, according to Charles Greville, who in his capacity as Clerk of the Council had no little to do in the necessary arrangements.

Equally satisfactory was the coronation of Queen Victoria. The enthusiasm over this event was in marked contrast with the lack of it in the case of that of George IV. Greville, writing on June 27th, 1838, says "There was never anything seen like the state of the town; it is as if the population had been on a sudden quintupled; the uproar, the confusion, the crowd, the noise, are indescribable. Horsemen, footmen, carriages, squeezed, jammed, intermingled, the pavement blocked up with timbers, hammering and knocking and falling fragments stunning the ears and threatening the head; not a mob here and there, but the town all mob, thronging, hustling, gaping and gazing at everything, at anything, at nothing. The park," he adds, "was a vast encampment; from the top of Piccadilly to the Abbey was one long line of scaffolding—very curious," he concludes, "but uncommonly tiresome, and the sooner it is over the better." On June 29th he writes: "The Coronation went off very well. The day was fine, without heat or rain—the innumerable multitude which thronged the streets orderly and satisfied." The procession of the state coaches of the Ambassadors and others produced a great effect, and the passing of the "sights self" was hailed vociferously. The young Queen had conquered the hearts even of those whom years of indifferent government had made ripe for rebellion. Inside the Abbey the scene must have been both impressive and affecting. The appearance of Marshall Soult, so long our military enemy; his conqueror, the Iron Duke, doing homage; the fall of Lord Rolle at the foot of the throne and the young Queen's rising to help him regain his feet, were, among many other incidents recorded by contemporary chroniclers, those that produced what the newspapers are fond of calling "sensation."

Over a period of fifty years, and fifty years which saw such extraordinary changes in manners and customs, it is impossible, within

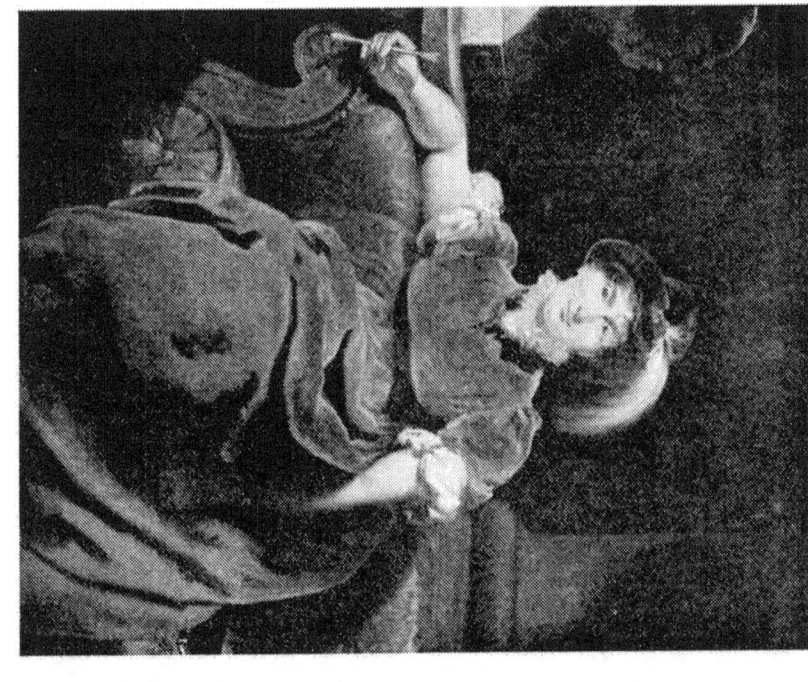

CAROLINE OF BRUNSWICK
From the Painting by Sir Thomas Lawrence

QUEEN VICTORIA IN 1839
From the Painting by Sully

PLATE 63

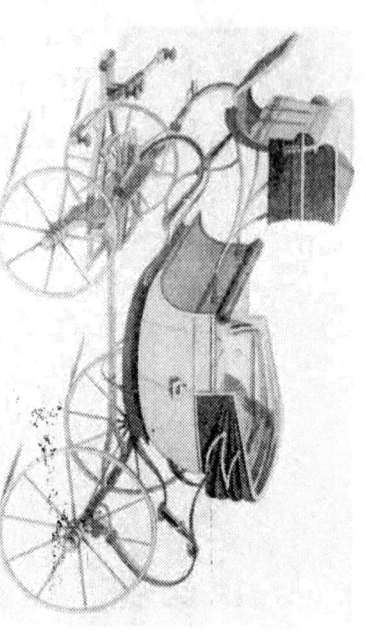

((a) Travelling Chariot; (b) Bretcha; (c) Landaulet; (d) Light Phaeton)

FASHIONABLE EQUIPAGES (1826)

PLATE 64

prescribed limits, to set down a tithe of the circumstances which may be said to have affected the daily life of the people. It must be remembered that the earlier years embraced such epoch-making events as the beginning and end of the great Napoleonic struggle. The effects of such things reflected themselves on the life of the people from the highest to the lowest, *mutatis mutandis*, as has the recent great war on our own generation. Indeed, allowing for the less complicated character of life generally during the earlier epoch, there is a great similarity between the state of the country when threatened by Napoleon and its condition when threatened by Pan-Germanism. The same feverish activity among civilians turned for the nonce into soldiers ; the departure of troops continually for the front ; the news of reverses and victories, the suspense, the heart-burning, the grief and pain. . . . .

After Waterloo London became a cosmopolitan city—gaiety and unrestrained joy took the place of anxiety, and even private grief found some measure of relief in the recognition of public safety. The great Duke (Plate 33) became the hero of the country and shared with the undying memory of Nelson, public regard and recognition. Wherever he went crowds followed him ; his house became one of the sights of the Town, and " No. 1, London " (Plate 2) was the first objective of the foreigner or the country cousin who came up to see the lions of the Metropolis ; while the Duke's funeral was one of those sights which have left a permanent memory behind them.

As time went on such excessive feelings gave place to more sober ones ; and in 1816 and 1819 the sufferings of the poor, due to reasons which always exist after great struggles, gave rise to considerable anxiety. If such things were more largely felt in the agricultural districts, the Londoner was not without his share of them. All sorts of events tended to give rise to apprehension. The Manchester Massacre was too far off to affect London except indirectly ; but the various Peace celebrations ; the assassination of Spencer Perceval ; the death of the Princess Charlotte in 1817 ; the Cato Street Conspiracy of February, 1820 ; the trial of Queen Caroline, which began in the following August, and her death and scandalously arranged funeral ; the news of Napoleon's end at St. Helena ; the disputes over the Catholic Emancipation Bill ; the death of Canning, which was regarded as a national loss ; and the destruction by fire of the Houses of Parliament in 1835 (Plate 15), and that of the Royal Exchange three years later, were all events which tended to excite the Londoner of the day and left their mark on the character of the people in general.

With the accession of William IV and the passing of the Reform Bill, a new era may be said to have been adumbrated, an era which was not wholly to be inaugurated until that day in June when the old king died at Windsor and the young girl, who was destined to reign so long, was hailed as our ruler, in the dim light of dawn, at Kensington Palace.

From the accession of Queen Victoria (Plate 63) to the death of Peel London may be said to have been gradually passing through that stage during which it threw off the Georgian Convention and thoroughly assimilated the Victorian. The wars that took place with China, Afghanistan, Scinde, and the rest, did not largely affect the life of a people to whom the great struggle nearer home was a recent memory. But such things as the trial of O'Connell, the great financial panic of 1847, and the Chartist riots of the following year left their impress on the London of the day; while such passing events as the Strawberry Hill sale[1] (1842), the disposal of the vast Stowe collections (1848), to each of which Londoners flocked in their thousands; the Eglinton Tournament of 1839, so amusingly parodied by Thackeray in " Cox's Diary "; the rise and development of the Railway Mania, with George Hudson as its protagonist,[2] excited that kind of momentary interest which had earlier been invoked by the Westminster Election and the arrest and trial of Sir Francis Burdett, whose house in Piccadilly was the centre of a popular demonstration when its owner was carried from it to the Tower.

Although riding and driving can hardly be included exactly under the headings of fun or frolic, because they were as much adjuncts to commercial necessity and health as to mere amusements, they can be more conveniently dealt with here than elsewhere in this volume. Both had an extraordinary vogue not only during the earlier years of the century but well on towards its close, although Gronow (writing in the sixties) bemoans the inferiority

[1] This disposal created amusement among the Philistines, and the egregious George Robins was parodied as Mr. Triptolemus Scattergoods, in a so-called catalogue of " Gooseberry Hill."

[2] Thackeray also refers to this in some of his lesser works, notably in " The Great Hoggarty Diamond " in which the West Diddlesex Corporation and its system was obviously based on some of the swindles arising out of the railway mania.

Sport and Politics: Rival Candidates Race Home with Voters during the Last Hour of an Election (circa 1820)

By R. Havell

A Meeting of the "Four-in-Hand Club" in Hyde Park (1838)

By James Pollard

PLATE 66

The Arrival of the Country Mails at the Gloucester Coffee-House, Piccadilly (1828)
By James Pollard

PLATE 67

THE LOUTH MAIL HELD UP BY THE SNOW (1836)
By James Pollard

TRAFFIC AT THE "ELEPHANT AND CASTLE," S.E. LONDON (circa 1820)
By Jones

PLATE 69

The New North-Western Railway: Excavating the Main Line at Camden Town

By J. C. Bourne

Entrance to the First Locomotive House at Camden Town

By J. C. Bourne

A General View of Bath in 1804

By J. C. Nattes

PLATE 71

THE PUMP-ROOM AT BATH (1804)

By J. C. Nattes

SYDNEY GARDENS, BATH (1804)

By J. C. Nattes

Brighton Pavilion: A Concert in the Music Room

By Joseph Nash

PLATE 73

BATH: A VIEW OF MILSOM STREET IN 1825
By Robert Cruikshank

CHELTENHAM: THE ENTRANCE TO THE ROYAL WELLS (1825)
By Robert Cruikshank

PROVINCIAL HEALTH RESORTS

On the Sands at Worthing (1808)

By John Nixon

FUN AND FROLIC

of the equipages as compared with those he remembered fifty years earlier. Then the Four-in-Hand Club was the theme of general admiration and " the spectacle of a grand turn-out of the members of that distinguished body was one of the glories of the days of the Regent " (Plate 66). The club, among whose original members were Lords Sefton, Barrymore, Worcester, and Fitzhardinge, Sir Henry Peyton, Sir John Lade, Major Forrester, Sir Bellingham Graham, and many another noted "whip" of the day, was accustomed to assemble in George Street, Hanover Square, and thence the coaches would set out for Salt Hill where a sumptuous dinner awaited the company, at the Windmill kept by the well-known host, Botham. In consequence of the death of many of its original members, the Club after an existence of some twenty years was broken up; but was soon after revived, as the result of a meeting held at Chesterfield House; and at a subsequent meeting at Richmond, on June 2nd, 1838, its new regulations were placed on a firm basis, and a new lease of life was given it. Lord Sefton, with his famous bays, was one of those who during the earlier period of the Club's career was a notable sight on the road; so was Lord Barrymore, whose skill as a whip equalled that of " Tommy Onslow"' and Sir John Lade, the latter of whom once drove a coach and four round the yard of Tattersalls.

Barrymore and Lade were both men who ought to have been born professional coachmen; in their get-up, their proficient use of slang and the phraseology of the stable, they were unrivalled, and the foreigner, Simond, who visited England in 1810, probably saw them on the occasion when he writes: " I have just seen the originals of which Matthews gave us a faithful copy a few days ago, in *Hit or Miss*—the very barouche club; the gentlemen-coachmen, with half-a-dozen great coats about them—immense capes—a large nosegay at the button-hole—high mounted on an elevated seat— with squared elbows—a prodigious whip—beautiful horses, four in hand, drive in a file to Salthill, a place about twenty miles from London, and return, stopping on the way at the several public-houses and gin shops where stage-coachmen are in the habit of stopping for a dram, and for parcels and passengers; the whole in strict imitation of their models and making use, as much as they can, of their energetic professional idiom." All this our observer says may be very amusing; but he adds, as a philosophical reflection, "Let these gentlemen remember that the lowering of the superior classes, the fashionable imitation of the vulgar, by people of superior rank in France, under the name of Anglo-mania, was one of the things that contributed to bring about the Revolution."

The tendency thus reprobated by M. Simond showed itself not only in relation to driving, however. The Marquis of Marylebone, in Disraeli's " Young Duke," is the type of the nobleman who loved to imitate his inferiors in dress, manner and language ; and during the Regency there were many who preferred hob-nobbing with stable hands, and finding amusement in the low haunts of the East-end, to consorting with their equals or mixing with the gay throng at Almack's. The consequence of a dissemination of such tastes showed itself in the coaching world, where the regular stage coaches were often tooled by illustrious noblemen who were as good in handling the ribbons as the professional coachmen, whose pupils they generally were.

The stage coaches which in those days linked up the provinces with the capital, much as railways were destined to do a few decades later, carried their loads of passengers and mails in every direction, and the great North Road, the Bath Road, the Dover Road, and the rest were busy with accumulated traffic (Plates 67 & 68). The inns on the various routes were centres of ceaseless activity, as the coaches and posting carriages arrived and left, and coachmen and guards, grooms and ostlers, were picturesque splashes of colour in the pictures of this phase of activity, which men like Herring, Alken, Pollard and Cruikshank have left us.

A whole literature has sprung up around the coaching days of the earlier part of the 19th century—a literature which has merged itself into the fiction of the period, and in which the practised hand of the great popular novelist of the day has created a sort of *hippic* apotheosis. In the pages of " Pickwick," and in some of the other novels that followed that middle-class epic, you can breathe the atmosphere of the road and hear the talk of the stable and the tap-room. The Dover Road lives again in those heroic pages and Old Weller emerges the type for all time of the stage-coachman of romantic fact. In Alken's inimitable pictures may you see the spanking team flying through a sunlit landscape, or haply engulfed in some tremendous snow-drift—that team which you saw with Cruikshank's eyes leaving the Whitehorse Cellar, or the Bolt in Tun, or, as in Pollard's picture, forming one of a regiment of others drawn up outside the General Post Office (Plate 80), ready to

FUN AND FROLIC

carry into all parts of the kingdom their human freight as well as their cargo of mails. De Quincey has given us the philosophy of the stage coach, just as Carlyle has left us a philosophy of clothes, and between the two we can gauge the characteristics of one of the most outstanding features of the pre-railway days, before Stephenson came and cast his iron girdle round the land and carried an urban influence into the very midst of a bucolicism desperately clinging to earlier manners, and customs.

By George Cruikshank.

Chapter VII.

HEALTH RESORTS.

When Mr. George Brummell determined to sell out of the 10th Hussars, the reason he gave to the Prince of Wales was that the regiment had been ordered to Manchester. " Manchester, Sir ! "—and he added " Besides you would not be there, Sir " ; whereupon the matter was settled. It would be doing a grave injustice to the second city in the kingdom, if one based one's judgment of it upon the Dandy's remark ; for although Manchester was a very different place then from what it is now, it was a centre of activity and increasing prosperity, just as it is now a centre of wealth and, if the horrid word may be allowed, of culture.

But there is no doubt that to one of Brummell's tastes and habits banishment to the north was unthinkable, and one is bound to say that contemporary accounts of Manchester confirm one's opinion that it was no place for a *persona grata* at Carlton House and an habitué of the clubs of St. James's Street. The fact that such a place would not have appealed to such a butterfly of fashion, is perhaps a point in its favour ; and certainly to regard it from a larger point of view will be to realise that it was taking the lead, even in those days, in the movement which produced the new provincial citizen and created the commercial backbone of the country. Its extraordinary growth may be realised by the fact that the place which Dr. Stukely had, in 1724, described as " the most rich, populous and busy *village* in England," had in 1801 no fewer than 84,000 inhabitants. But it was still governed by a Boroughreeve and two Constables, and preserved many of those older forms of self-government which did well enough while a place was, so to speak, finding itself.

Its amusements were largely local. But the Theatre and Music were even then well represented. Indeed, a contemporary writer says, not untruly, that " the Manchester stage can boast of being a nursery for those in London," and we know that such leading lights as Miss Farren, Mrs. Siddons, Kemble, Cooke, and Munden were all regularly engaged performers at the Theatre Royal, which, in 1800, was under the management of Bellamy, the Incledon of Dublin, as he has been called.

A Regatta in Dover Harbour (circa 1830)
From a Contemporary Drawing

PLATE 75

PLATE 76

BRIGHTON: A VIEW OF THE STEYNE IN 1825
By Robert Cruikshank

COWES: THE PROMENADE DURING REGATTA-TIME (1825)
By Robert Cruikshank

SEASIDE RESORTS

HEALTH RESORTS

Billiards then as now was a favourite form of recreation, and there was a regular saloon open from 8 in the morning in summer and from 9 in the winter till 10 at night. Some of its regulations seem strange in these times. For instance, the price of a single game by day was 3d., by *candlelight* 6d., no one was permitted to bet more than 2s. 6d. on a game ; no liquor was allowed in the room.

There was also a regular Concert Room which had been erected in 1777, "lighted by elegant glass chandeliers," and here, to use the words of one writing in 1804, "the numerous assemblage of fair ' Lancashire witches ' listening to the ' Concord of sweet sounds ' from the parterre and gallery, afford a rich treat to the eyes of the admirers of female beauty, whilst the lovers of harmony are gratified by the excellence of both amateur and professional performers."

The Circus in Chatham Street may be regarded as a wholly local attraction, but the Races, which were held annually at Whitsuntide, on Kersal Moor, attracted crowds from all parts. Among these crowds were numbers of beggars, which the annual Fair, held about the same time, drew to the place ; but a law enacted in 1804, providing for the lodging of many of these in the New Bailey Prison, helped to mitigate what is described as a shocking nuisance.

Although Manchester was thus relatively exiguous in the earlier years of the century, many things happened there which laid the foundation for its present prosperity. It was the £100,000 left by John Owens in 1846 that started the great University ; in 1838 the city received its Charter of Incorporation ; in 1847 it became a Bishop's See ; in 1829 the Manchester and Liverpool[1] Railway had been opened, on which occasion William Huskisson so tragically lost his life.

It was indeed the great system of railway travelling thus inaugurated, to be followed by the Liverpool and Birmingham Line opened in 1837 ; and the London and Birmingham Railway, 1838 ; as well as the fact that by 1840 there were 838 miles of rails in various parts of the country, which gradually drove the old coaches off the road, and brought all kinds of centres nearer the Metropolis ; although in early days the trains led by " Puffing Billy " travelled not faster than 15 miles an hour !

Of the old coaching routes one of the most popular was that to

---

[1] It was at the Theatre Royal, Liverpool, it will be remembered, that Palmer died on the stage while acting in " The Stranger,"

LIFE IN REGENCY AND EARLY VICTORIAN TIMES

Bath, when the light four-inside Fast Coaches of about 1823, marked the meridian of road travelling. That journey past Reading and Newbury, Marlborough and Devizes, was one of the most picturesque of these old coach routes, and luckily so, for probably more people went to Bath (many of them, of course, posting in their own equipages) than anywhere else, till fashion and proximity made Brighton famous. The glory of Bath really passed with the 18th century, but as it still held its own as a health resort, as it does to-day, it must be regarded as the chief of those spas where the jaded Londoner seeks re-invigoration or the retired Army man seeks repose. At the beginning of the century it may be said to have reached the zenith of its fame, and a certain glory still clung about the place, a glory reflected from the times of Nash and Fielding and Smollett, a glory which will never quite disappear, one imagines (Plates 70 & 71). But its day of real splendour was over, and those who came to Bath came now chiefly to benefit by its waters rather than to benefit by its fashionable atmosphere; so that by the middle of the century it had become the Bath of the hypochondriac and the gouty, and no longer specially a resort of the *haut ton*.

The feelings of its former *habitués* in this respect are reflected in poetical effusions, such as that produced by Mr. Pratt, about 1800; and may be traced in the veracious history of Mr. Pickwick. In 1807 the Lower Assembly Rooms, where the great Nash had rebuked duchesses, was advertised as to be let; people began rather to entertain in their own houses than to seek the mixed society of the public réunions. In Jane Austen's novels one can read between the lines that there was a waning tendency in that Bathomania which had so virulently attacked an earlier generation, and it is evident that Bath society was becoming so mixed that the better classes were forming cliques and setting a pattern of ultra-exclusiveness. It is obvious that Angelo Cyrus Bantam, Esq., M.C., was but a poor substitute for the gorgeous and dignified Nash, and could only patronise a class of persons whom his prototype would never even have permitted to enter his reception rooms.

About the 'thirties a new era was beginning in Bladud's city; from being one of temporary fashionable resort, it was merging into one of respectable permanent residence; and although its former characteristic has never quite deserted it, it remains to-day, what the earlier half of the last century made it—a retiring ground for

HEALTH RESORTS

old military men and maiden ladies, who in its delightful 18th century setting somehow contrive to preserve an old world air hardly to be found anywhere else in England. Everyone who was anyone had been to Bath, not so often perhaps as Mr. Wilberforce who came here no fewer than 18 times, from his first visit to Mr. Pitt, in 1782, to his last, in the year of his death, 1833. Indeed, down roughly to 1840 it was usual for many to spend a month here preparatory to the London season, and few of the great coaching roads were so frequented as that which connected the two cities.[1] If those who were to be seen loitering in the Orange Grove or strolling up Milsom Street (Plate 73) and about the purlieus of Queen's Square, were attracted hither rather by considerations of health than of fashion, their presence gave distinction to a place that has never wholly lacked distinction. Here might have been seen the gaunt form of Mr. Pitt passing stately to the Pump Room (1806); here the old world figure of Governor Pownall (he died February, 1805, in Bath); that curious adventuress, Caraboo, Princess of Jarasa, as she styled herself, here created something of a sensation in 1817, as Mrs. Piozzi tells us; here, according to the same gossip, Queen Charlotte drove all the society of Bath distracted by her arrival in the same year—being received with alarums and excursions: "the illumination more gaudy than I ever saw London exhibit," exclaims Dr. Johnson's old friend. It was in Bath Abbey that the Rev. Legh Richmond preached on "Cruelty to Animals," in 1802, and "excited much notice." Hither in 1827 came Queen Adelaide, and three years later the Victoria Park was opened by the Princess Victoria at the mature age of eleven, in which Park a column was set up on the occasion of her accession in 1837.

All this time Bath was increasing in size and receiving all sorts of improving touches. Churches and banks, hospitals and other benevolent institutions, were springing up; old buildings were being demolished, what time Mr. Wilberforce continued to visit here, and Landor received Dickens, and Beckford still collected bric-à-brac and books. Beckford's name is an outstanding one in Bath, and indeed with his passing in 1844, and the sale of his famous tower in 1847, the transition period of Bath's history may be said to have closed; that period which linked up the hoops and patches and Sedan

---

[1] Apart from many books on coaching, which include this highway, its topographical features have been preserved by Robertson in his "Great Bath Road," 2 vols., 1792.

LIFE IN REGENCY AND EARLY VICTORIAN TIMES

chairs of the 18th century, with its poke bonnets and its strapped trousers, and the mail coaches of the 19th—a period dominated by the rotund figure of Mr. Pickwick, whose namesake ran the coach in which the immortal once travelled.

One of the reasons for the decline of Bath as a fashionable resort was the ever-increasing popularity of Brighton. Brighton has a position apart among such resorts, and of the places that flourished during the earlier years of the 19th century, none is quite so pregnant with memories as this favourite haunt of George, Prince of Wales. The Brighthelmstone which Doctor Johnson found so dull, and whose downs he considered so desolate " that if one had a mind to hang one's self for desperation at being obliged to live there, it would be difficult to find a tree on which to fasten the rope," and where Gibbon and Fanny Burney found the air so invigorating and the retirement so restful, had in the course of a few years emerged into a place of distinction under royal *ægis*.

The Duke of Cumberland was the originating cause of the Prince's patronage of Brighton. He and his duchess were here in 1782, and in the following year Prince ' Florizel ' came to pay him a visit. He stayed over a week and derived so much benefit from the bathing and the air that he came again the next year. The inhabitants, very much alive to the advantages of having the Heir Apparent among them as much as possible, did all in their power to get him to become a resident, and it was probably as the result of many intricate and delicate manœuvres that Weltje, the Prince's major-domo, became possessed of a freehold piece of land, and in 1787 made over a twenty-one year's lease of it to his royal master. This was the origin of that Pavilion which was a-building any time from 1802 to 1820, and which remains to-day probably the most characteristic memento of the Regency period of which it is the crowning absurdity (Plates 1 & 72). But it is unfair to make a cock-shy of the poor old thing in its days of decadence, and in recent times it has been of material use. It is said that the gift of some Chinese wall papers which he received, turned the Prince's mind to this special kind of architectural phantasy. It may be so, but an oriental taste was in the air, it having been introduced by Sir William Chambers on his return from China, as may be seen in many of the decorations of great houses and in much of the furniture made by Chippendale at this period. But with the exception of the Kew Pagoda no other structure had actually been

HEALTH RESORTS

contrived in this form before,—as Sydney Smith once said, "St. Paul's had come to Brighton and pupped."

The Prince was vastly pleased with it, and we know that Mr. Turveydrop thought it a prodigious fine building. It resumes in itself the Brighton of George the Illustrious. There he received his friends who were constantly driving down to see him, as he himself used to drive down, and who made the Steyne (Plate 76), in spite of Mrs. Fitzherbert's efforts to preserve decorum, anything but decent or decorous. The company which the Prince assembled here was much the same as might, at other seasons, have been met at Carlton House: Brummell and Barrymore, Colonel Hanger and Sir John Lade and the rest, with hangers-on of both sexes and often of more than doubtful reputation. Indeed, the Pavilion is the focus round which the fashionable records of Brighton radiate. The Prince's life there seems to have been passed alternately in walking on the Steyne daily, attended by his satellites; going to concerts, the play, or the balls which were held with frequency at the Castle. His kindness and condescension and general urbanity made him friends among all classes, from the tradesmen he ruined to the inhabitants he so often scandalised. Many of the humbler denizens have become famous through their connection with the royal host of the Pavilion—" Smoaker " Miles, the sailor, and Martha Gunn, the bathing woman; Phœbe Hessel, who had once served as a private and had fought at Fontenoy, and the rest who bulk largely in local annals and are not unknown in the history of the larger world, in company with such noble and leading lights as Alvanley and the " Jockey of Norfolk."

By the end of the first decade of the century Brighton had become the most fashionable resort in England, and if many of the more sedate inhabitants were driven away by the wild doings of the Prince's set, the bulk of the population,[1] especially the tradespeople, hailed the royal presence with a joy born of dreams of endless patronage and consequent prosperity. They even set up a statue of the Prince, carved by Rossi in 1802, a statue of plaster which became damaged and for which Chantrey's bronze figure in the Steyne was substituted in 1828.

For the accommodation of the Dandies who drove down and stayed at the Pavilion or at the inns, Raggett of White's opened

[1] In 1761 there were 472 people in Brighton, in 1801, 1,233; by 1831 the number had grown to 7,740.

a club-house on the Steyne, about whose purlieus all sorts of weird figures were to be seen, among them " Romeo " Coates and the Baron de Geramb, and that Henry Cope—the " Green Man "— whose clothes and even hair were dyed to this verdant hue. Mrs. Fitzherbert lived on the Steyne, and her presence checked in some measure the Prince's wild doings. Sheridan sometimes came down, and Warren Hastings, and these two former antagonists were actually introduced to each other at a dinner at the Pavilion. But the society and notable visitors were not wholly of the Prince's set. Rogers had a small house off the Parade in 1808 ; Charles Lamb and his sister were here rather later ; Lord Mansfield rented a house on the Steyne, where Burke once stayed with him. Canning was another visitor, and Sir Philip Francis ; while the Creeveys used to run down, and on one occasion at the Pavilion Mrs. Creevey had quite an unpleasant time, as readers of her husband's diary will remember. More illustrious visitors were the Emperor of Russia and the King of Prussia, in 1814, and twice Queen Charlotte came to see her son here ; on the second occasion being accompanied by the Princess Charlotte. The Prince once even brought down his royal wife, the Princess Caroline !

All this time, by a process of successive additions, the Pavilion was assuming that appearance which it possesses to-day ; and the amount of money that was spent on that exotic toy must have been enormous. Other attractions were Mahomed's Baths, the Assembly Rooms, and Fisher's Library ; and Brighton copied Bath by having a duly elected Master of the Ceremonies, in the person of Captain Wade (succeeded in 1808 by one Forth), and rang its bells on the arrival of important visitors, as they had done in the city of Bladud under Nash. The Ship and the Castle were the two chief hotels, but in the course of time the latter was bought by the Regent and incorporated in the Pavilion grounds. The fact that people went from Brighton to Dieppe (Haydon and Wilkie did so in 1814) as a cheaper though longer route to the Continent than by way of Dover and Calais, gave the place the added bustle of a sea-port ; and the presence in the neighbourhood of military camps brought another section of society, a section in which Lydia Bennet and the Osbornes and Rawdon Crawleys found themselves much in their element. Yet other attractions were the Brighton Races ; the cricket matches, in which Colonel Hanger and Lord Darnley used to distinguish themselves ; the cock-pit which was to be found by the initiated in the White Hart; and, even in 1810, the bull-baiting which took place at Hove; while all sorts of shows, from prize-fighting to the weird and wonderful wagers instituted by the Pavilion set, could be witnessed by the populace at large, and helped to enhance the daily round of pleasure or excitement.

The promenade on the Steyne was chiefly patronised during the evening, the "genteel hour" being 9 o'clock; but the theatre was a counter attraction—that theatre which, since the days when Mrs. Siddons graced its boards, till our time, has been *sui generis* in attracting all the greatest exponents of the art.

George, Prince of Wales, made Brighton, but at his death its popularity was not materially affected. It had become so firmly established in public favour that it was henceforth, as it were, able to run by itself. In 1827 he visited the place for the last time, and he is said to have abandoned it at the instance of Lady Conyngham, who had been offended by some act of the Brightonians. But the royal dukes continued to come down, and in 1830 William IV spent Christmas at the Pavilion, making much, as he always did, of Mrs. Fitzherbert, who lived, till her death in 1837, in her house on the Steyne in a sort of semi-regal state.

Greville describes Brighton in 1832, as being then gay, amusing and bustling. Indeed, it seems to have proved too much so for Queen Victoria, who having found the inhabitants "indiscreet," never visited the place after 1843. It was in the following year, however, that the Prince of Wales, with his young brothers and sisters, stayed at the Pavilion, that being the last time it was to house royalty.

In 1849 an Act of Parliament was passed for the sale of "Florizel's Folly," and the Town exercised the option it had obtained to purchase the property. With this closes that period of Brighton's history embracing the period here under review.

Although it would be impossible to give a list of a tithe of the notable people who came here for more or less extended visits during these days, one may mention one or two outstanding names, such as those of the Misses Berry, Horace Smith, Harriet Mellon (once Mrs. Coutts and later Duchess of St. Albans), the "Mrs. Million" of "Vivian Grey." Campbell and Crabb-Robinson were visitors as, too, was Scott in 1828, staying with the Lockharts; Rogers and Theodore Hook, Leech and Copley Fielding, Disraeli,

Mark Lemon, Sydney Smith, Macready, and Dickens, who "did not approve of Brighton in the abstract," but who wrote some of "Oliver Twist" here, and here found the prototype of Mrs. Pipchin.

But it was Thackeray who was Brighton's great *laudator*. Hither he came frequently and here, at the Ship, he wrote a chapter of "Vanity Fair"; and we have little doubt but that it was that chapter (25) in which "All the principal personages think fit to leave Brighton," in which Becky Sharp's " bright green eyes streamed out and shot into the night "; in which George Osborne fell under their baleful influence; in which Emmy was neglected and unhappy.

If we wish to get some general idea of what such important places as, say Liverpool and Birmingham, Oxford and Cambridge, Bristol and Norwich or York[1], were like during the first half of the 19th century, we must rely on such impressions as they conveyed to foreign travellers—Louis Simond or Goede, for instance, rather than resort to the contemporary guide books, which are full of data as to new public buildings and the inauguration of philanthropic institutions, but which leave social life severely alone. The fact is that they were all beginning that tremendous growth largely under the influence of the birth of scientific discovery with which the names of Stephenson and James Watt, Cavendish and Dalton, and Priestley and so many others, are identified. Many of these places still preserved features of antiquity which the progress of ideas and the increase of population had not yet affected, just as smaller places were still clad in the air of an earlier day, as we see in Turner's delightful picture of Dartford, which for all the world might have been drawn in the earlier years of the preceding century. The gradual development of ideas, the changes in dress and in manners and customs which we have seen characterising the capital, made themselves felt in the other great centres of life. Linked up with London, first by the coaches and then by the ever increasing system of railways, these places gradually reflected the varying fashions of the Metropolis, and thus became in course of time self-sufficing centres, and more and more independent of exoteric influence. None of them could claim to be fashionable in the sense that Bath had been and Brighton actually was, and thus from our present point of view they are not so important as even Ramsgate

[1] York Races were very popular at this time; and it was at York that Mrs. Thornton rode her famous race against Flint, on August 25th, 1804, when the latter won amidst great excitement, a circumstance that occasioned a fracas between Colonel Thornton, the lady's husband, and Flint. In the following year Mrs. Thornton beat Buckle in a similar race.

Netted Silk Bags

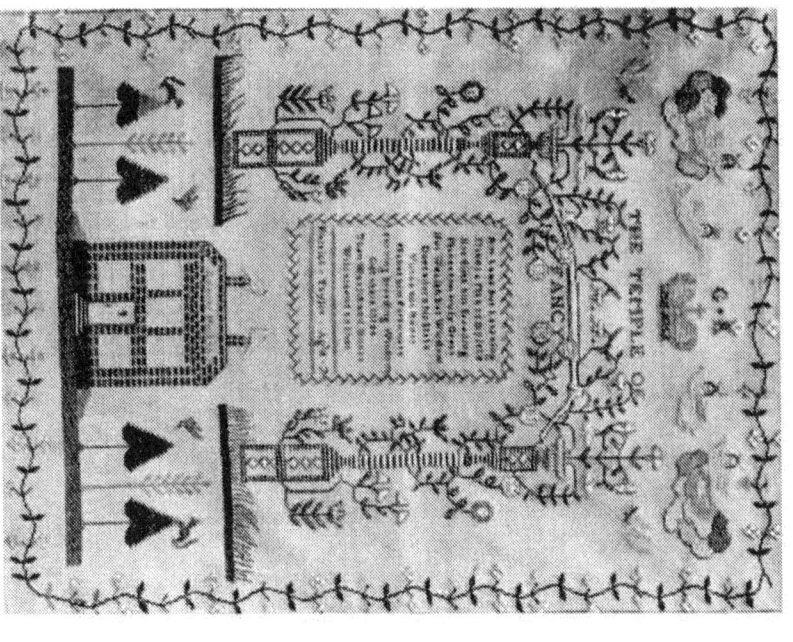

A Stitched Sampler

EARLY VICTORIAN HANDICRAFTS

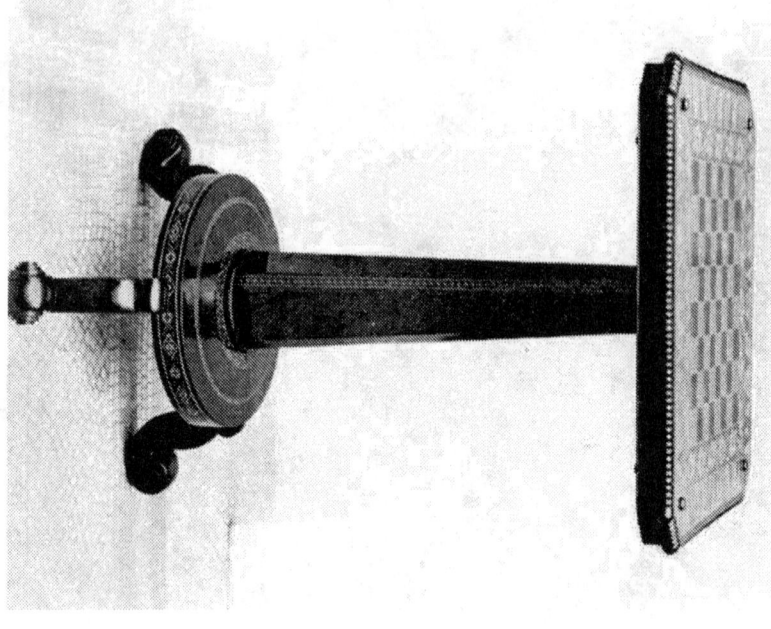

Chess Table with Marquetry Top
(Tonbridge Ware)

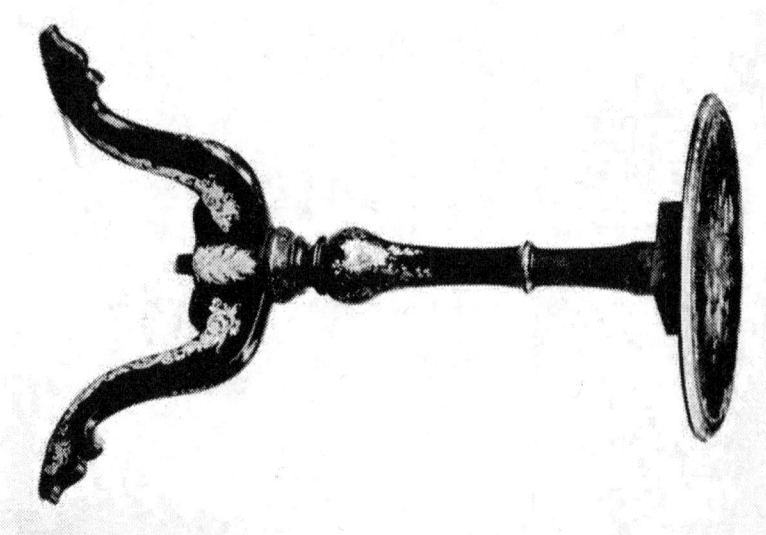

Tripod Table with Floral
Mother-of-Pearl Inlay

EARLY VICTORIAN FURNITURE

PLATE 78

HEALTH RESORTS

and Margate, which about this time were beginning their careers as favourite summer resorts.

Hastings, Eastbourne, and Worthing (Plate 74) were, too, much in favour, and Weymouth and Sidmouth had already a certain vogue due to the patronage of George III, who derived benefit from the air of the former place. Racing drew crowds on certain occasions to Doncaster and Newmarket; hunting (Plate 22) made Melton[1] then as now a great centre of sport. Yachting (Plates 75 & 76) as well as its salubrious (to use a word favoured at that time) air, brought the Isle of Wight into fashion, and Malvern and Cheltenham vied with Bath in attracting the valetudinarian. In the pages of "The English Spy," and particularly in the illustrations (Plates 73 & 76) which Robert Cruikshank contributed to that curious work, you may read, allusively enough it is true, of the doings of both the "ton" and the lower stratas of society in these various haunts, and here you can get quite a good idea of the general aspect of the social life of the period as it was reflected in these places.

There was also another centre which rivalled these and remained for many years a fashionable retiring place for the Londoner, I mean Tunbridge Wells. The Tunbridge Wells of the 19th century could hardly claim to be what it was at an earlier period when Beau Nash had shed the light of his countenance upon it, or when the masculine-minded Princess Amelia was accustomed to patronise it; when Gray and Young and Richardson had there met the Chudleighs and the Montagus, and when Lady Lincoln and the Duchess of Norfolk could be seen walking on the Pantiles with Dr. Johnson and Colley Cibber. But, as at Bath, fashion died hard in the Kentish Spa, and, together with the owners of illustrious names in the Peerage, might have been noted the sepulchral visage of Rogers and the homely countenance of Mary Lamb, and her famous brother. Mary Berry used to stay there, and thus linked up the fashion and literature of two centuries; while Lydia White and Luttrell, and, later, Thackeray, who wrote his charming Roundabout, entitled "Tunbridge Toys," there, carried on the literary traditions of the place. There is no doubt, too, that the lengthy sojourns of the Duke of Sussex and, still more, the not infrequent visits of the Duchess of Kent and the Princess Victoria, gave it a fashionable air that often does more for a place than salubrity of climate or picturesqueness of environment.

[1] Melton was the headquarters of cock-fighting, and in the vicinity a race of birds was bred specially for this kind of sport.

LIFE IN REGENCY AND EARLY VICTORIAN TIMES

Tunbridge Wells is to-day a much built-over place, but it yet retains an air of Regency and early Victorian days in a greater degree, perhaps, than any other town in England. There the railway seems something of an anachronism. One should always arrive posting or by coach, just as one should at Bath. But architectural features will always stamp the larger place as essentially of the 18th century; whereas in the smaller the houses one sees, except those produced by later building development, are eloquent of the day when the Prince Regent ruled the land or when the young Queen had caught up in her inexperienced but plastic fingers, the reins of governance. Probably nothing in Tunbridge Wells is so capable of recalling its earlier days, at least those passed in budding Victorian years, as the specimens of Tunbridge ware which are to be found in curiosity shops and in many houses where the aroma of that period still prevails. We all know those work-boxes and what-nots composed of hard wood inlaid with black and brown and buff designs, which are as sentient of the era as are those groups of coloured wax fruits, carefully shielded under glass cases, or those black tables and tea-trays on which flowers of gaudy hues, whose brilliance is still further heightened by impossible leaves of inlaid mother-of-pearl, are meticuously painted (Plate 78).

There is, to-day, quite a vogue for these examples of the early Victorian convention. The time was one of short cuts to effect in needlework, and the bead purses and bags which are now sought after prove the industry, if not exactly the artistic capabilities, of their makers (Plate 77). Painted fire-screens exercised the leisure of many a young lady in the intervals of her archery (Toxophilite Clubs were *de rigueur* (Plate 22)—that founded by Sir Ashton Lever, of "Museum" fame, in 1781, received the title "Royal" in 1847), her ride in the Row, or her perusal of some carefully selected romance. Screens of a different sort, those composed of scraps, engravings or coloured prints, were another resource of those of leisure, fortified with scissors and paste. The construction of dolls was a favourite pastime of the young, often graciously assisted by their elders, and in the London Museum may be seen quite an army of little puppets dressed by Princess Victoria with the help of Mlle. Lehzen.

Many of these things were not exactly new, but were offshoots from what had been done in the same direction in the preceding century. But just as that century was more picturesque in most of its manifestations than its successor, so the dolls and the dolls houses and the needlework, from samplers to elaborate chair covers of the succeeding century, were lacking in the earlier distinction. Crudeness of colour became fashionable. Positive hues, such as emerald greens and dazzling scarlets and Bakst-like magentas (so many of which are, to-day, having a recrudescence) were favourably regarded. Baxter prints had a vogue, not, as now, as rarities collected and guarded jealously, but as illustrations to books and as decorations to nurseries where children were kept in their place under a rather jailer-like surveillance.

Indeed, Mrs. Pipchin ruled among the budding generation, and Paul Dombey and Florence and the rest, unreal as they and their outlook may seem to us now, when the child is indeed father of the man, were really then typical of the young idea. Youngsters look, to-day, with disdain on the little books full of wise saws and modern instances which the " dear papa " or the " dear mamma " presented to their off-spring with highly moral sentiments inscribed on the fly-leaves; laughter is created by the epistolary effusions of the little boys and girls of the period who were the " obliged and affectionate " sons or daughters of their dear parents. The curious thing is that, treated very much as children in a sort of affectionate *de haut en bas* manner by their elders, the young men seem so often to have been in their manners and ways like little old men and women. The youthful Macaulay is, of course, an exceptional example with his " Thank you, Madame, the pain is abated," and his uncanny knowledge of Holy Writ;[1] but if in an exaggerated way he was symptomatic of his age—an age in which the youths of both sexes were dressed not so much like children as like miniature replicas of their parents—, and the childish, delightful little creatures clad in flowing, easy garments, and full of the *joie de vivre*, whom we encounter in the pictures of Reynolds and Gainsborough, Hoppner and Raeburn, had turned into the rather stilted, uncomfortably dressed youngsters who look out on us from a thousand canvasses which the hack portraitists of the day produced and had the audacity to charge for as works of art.

The background to all this is to be found in the solid substantial houses in which our forbears dwelt amongst furniture as solid and as heavy. The puritan revival was in full force, and it is suggestive

[1] See, too, a letter from him to Hannah More, dated January 16th, 1815, when he was but 15, given in " Letters of H. More to Zachary Macaulay," published in 1860.

that what with Georgian directness was called a wine-cooler, was, by the early Victorians, designated a sarcophagus! One can, to-day, enter houses where the old convention lingers, in which the whole period seems still to be focussed, and of which Thackeray's descriptions, in "Vanity Fair" and the "Roundabout Papers," still hold good. The massive chairs, the overwhelming bookcases, from which the graces of the Adams and Chippendale and Sheraton have been for ever banished, the sideboard solid like cast iron veneered with mahogany, the ponderous red curtains to keep out the light, and the expensive carpets to harbour the dust! It was a poor exchange for the light and grace that had preceded it, and yet—so powerful is distance in adding enchantment—even such things as I have here attempted to adumbrate, have through the *series annorum* come to possess an attraction; and as we are going back, under the direction of our artistic advisers, to the blatant colours which the æstheticism of the 'eighties had, one almost thought, banished for ever, and the super-sensitiveness of the 'nineties had made hateful, so in the matter of furniture there are tendencies of a return to the early Victorian convention. People no longer turn up their noses at the massiveness of pure mahogany; they positively fight for ebonized tables bearing their bouquets of flowers and mother-of-pearl; they collect and even carry in the light of day, the bead purses of their grandmothers, and in spite of Cartier, in spite of Arts and Crafts, ponderous earrings and the jewellery compact of much gold and congregated turquoises, are not disdained.

What has happened is obvious. The first half of the 19th century, having fulfilled its destiny as a living thing, has become historic and slightly legendary. We are now regarding it as those of fifty years ago regarded the 18th century. Its manners and customs, its houses and its furniture, its art and its music, are coming back to us as among those far-off things which carry their halo of antiquity about them and which wreathed in the mist of the past, are clothing themselves anew in our mind's-eye with romance and something of mystery. And so if we have become too sophisticated wholly to throw ourselves into that past again, we can at least reconstruct it, and in doing so can look back upon it with amusement and with interest; perhaps, sometimes, with a recurring wonder not untouched by envy and even regret.

PLATE 79

A REVIEW OF TROOPS IN HYDE PARK BY THE PRINCE REGENT AND THE ALLIED SOVEREIGNS *From a Contemporary Print*

THE OPENING OF THE GRAND JUNCTION CANAL AT PADDINGTON
By H. Milbourne

THE QUEEN'S NEW STEAM YACHT AT A REVIEW AT SPITHEAD
From a Contemporary Drawing

Mail Coaches Leaving the General Post-Office (1830)

By James Pollard

INDEX TO TEXT AND ILLUSTRATIONS

The Figures in heavy type refer to Plate Numbers of Illustrations.

	PAGE
Ackermann	20
Albert Hall	39
Albert, Prince, influence of	7
Aiken, Henry, Cockpit	40
,, Driving a Tandem	38
,, Steeplechasing	**52**, 108
Almack's	**5, 6, 27, 28, 34, 38,** 49-58
Alvanley, Lord	**26,** 29
Amusements	**2, 3, 21, 22,** 37, 38, **57,** 87-109, 110
Apperley, portrait by Maclise	19
Archer	23, 120
Archery Meeting	**22**
Architecture of the period	12, **8, 31, 32, 39,** 77
Arnold, Matthew	11
Art, generally	70-77
Ascot	30, **54,** 90
Atkinson, J. A., Punch and Judy	57
Bagnigge Wells	94
Balfe, M. W.	**45,** 82, 83
Ballooning	95
Barry	73
Bartholomew Fair	100, 101
Bartolozzi, F.	54
Bassie, Master	55
Bath, general view (1804)	70
,, Pump-room	71
,, Sydney Gardens	71
,, Milsom Street	73, 192 ff.
Baxter prints	77, 121
Bayswater Tea Gardens	95
Beadwork	77, 120
Bear-fights	87
Beechey, Sir William	71
Bennett, Sterndale	82, 83

	PAGE
Betting, see Gambling.	
Betty, Master	86
Bishop, Henry	82
"Blackmantle"	6
Blake, T., A Sparring Match	51
Blake, William	11
Blessington, Lady, portraits	**3, 25,** 7, **32, 33, 44, 45,** 45, 46
Blücher, General, mobbed	8
"Bobbies"	2
Bonington, R. P.	11
,, Rouen after	**42,** 70
Botanic Gardens	19
Bourne, J. C., drawings after	69
Bow Street Runners	61
Boxing	50, 51, 88, 89
Boys, T. S.	23, 34
,, Reproductions of drawings	**14, 34, 37**
Briggs, H. P., portrait of Sydney Smith	**45**
Brighton, view of the Old Steyne	76
,, the Pavilion	**1, 114, 115**
Brontë, sisters	11, 54
Brooks, H., Burton's Archway to Hyde Park	**2**
Brooks's Club, interior	30, **49,** 63
Browning, Robert	11
Brummell, Beau (George)	6, 14
,, from a miniature	18
,, in retirement	19, 24, 34, 59, 63, 64, 119
Bucks, the, exploits depicted	20
,, described	93
Bull-baiting	117
Bull-fighting	87
Burton, Decimus	1
,, W. Entrance to Hyde Park	**2**

INDEX

Byng, "Poodle," portrait by Dighton - 19, 26
Byron, Lord - 11

Callcott, Sir A. W. - 74
Canaletto - 23
Card-players, depicted by H. Moses - 21
    by Rowlandson - 27
Carlyle, Thomas - 78, 81, 82
Caroline of Brunswick (Queen) 2, 8, 48, 63, 89, 103, 104, 116
Castlereagh, Lady - 51
Castlereagh, Lord - 10
Catalani, Angelica - 47, 83
Chalon, A. E., Two Prima Donnas - 47
Chantrey, Sir Francis - 11
  ,, Self-portrait - 43
  ,, Portrait of Scott - 44, 72
Charity Bazaar (1832) - 55
Charleville, Lady - 47
"Charlies" - 20, 2
Charlotte, Princess - 40, 105, 115
Chartists, the - 8, 106
Chelsea - 19
  ,, the Bun House - 98
  ,, C. Embankment, after Parrott - 13
Cheltenham, Royal Wells - 73
Children - 10, 121
Chimney-sweeps - 57
Chiswick House, *after* Shepherd 36, 48
Chloroform - 8
Chopin, F., in England - 84
Class distinctions - 35*ff*, 54
Classic art - 15, 76, 77
Clubs - 5, 64*ff*
Coaching - 5, 108, 109, 111, 112
Cock and Hen Clubs - 37
Cock-fighting 87, 89, 116, 117, 119
Cock-pit, depicted by Alken - 40
  ,, described - 61
Coffee-house - 5
  ,, *after* Lane - 27
Coleridge, S. T. - 11

Collins, William - 74
Colour in dress, etc. 7, 8, 28, 31, 121
Concerts - 54
  ,, in Brighton Pavilion 72, 103
  ,, in Manchester - 111
Constable, John - 11, 70, 72
Cooke, "Kangaroo" - 27
Coronation ceremonies - 2, 103, 104
  ,, of George IV - 61, 62
Cotman, J. S. - 70
Cowes, *after* R. Cruikshank - 76
Cowper, W. - 11
Cox, David - 11, 70
Crabbe, George - 11, 78
Crawford, "Teapot" - 26
Creevey, Thomas, *quoted* - 60
Cremorne, entrance to - 59, 97
Creswick, Thomas - 71
Cricket - 91, 92, 116
Crimping - 10
Crockford's, gaming room at - 30, 61
Crome, John, Poringdale Oak - 42
Crosby Hall - 84
Crotch, Dr. William - 82
Cruikshank, George - 12, 32, 34
  ,, Dancing at Almack's 38
  ,, entr'acte at Covent Garden - 47
  ,, fashions and frights 38
  ,, Green Room at Drury Lane - 49, 57, 58, 74, 93, 101, 108, 109
Cruikshank, Robert, Brooks's Club, interior - 30
  ,, Gaming room at Crockford's - 30
  ,, Cowes during Regatta - 76
  ,, View of the Steyne, Brighton - 76
  ,, Milsom Street, Bath - 73, 119

Daguerre, L. J. - 72
Danbrava, H. de, portrait of Wellington - 33

INDEX

	PAGE
Dancing	49, 50
" at Almack's	5, 38
Dandies	24*ff*
" literary	78, 79, 103
" "low" tastes of	108
Davies, Lady Clementine	50
De Quincey, Thomas	81
Derby, the	90
" the Derby Winner	41
De Wint, Peter	11, 70, 77
Dighton, R., London Nuisances	6, 72
Dickens, Charles	11, 13, 17, 33, 54, 79, 80, 81, 101, 118
Dilettante Dinner, *after* Shepherd	46
"Directoire" style in architecture	32
Disraeli, Benjamin	33
" portrait by Maclise	35
" *quoted*	62, 79
Dog-fighting	89
Doll-making	120, 121
Doncaster	90
D'Orsay, the Count	6, 7, 24
" portrait	25, 33, 26, 32, 52, 59, 64, 72
Dover Regatta, (c 1830)	75
Downman, John	71
Doyle, Richard	12, 74, 101
Dramatic Critics	85
Dress	2, 13, 28, 31, 74, 121
See also Fashions.	
Driving	106, 107
" tandem	38
Drummond, George	64
Duelling	10
Early Victorianism	13, 24*ff*
Eastlake, Sir C. L.	74
Edgworth, Maria	11
Egan, Pierce	5, 6, 14, 41
Election Incidents	56, 65
Elgin Marbles	77
Eliot, George	11
Epsom	30, 90
" Betting Ring at	52

	PAGE
Equipages	58, 64
Etty, William	74
Fashions for 1839	24
Fashion and Folly *after* Heath	11, 11a
Fashion and Custom	25, 74
Field, John	82
Fielding, Copley	11, 7p, 77
Fire-engines	2
Firescreens	120
Fireworks	8, 95, 96, 97, 103
Fitzherbert, Mrs., portrait *after* Cosway	18, 115, 117
Fives Court, interior	51, 89
Flaxman, John	11
Football	91
Four-in-hands	29, 36
" Club, in Hyde Park	66, 107
Fox, C. J.	659
Franking of letters	17
Fraser, Sir William, *quoted*	53
"Free and Easys"	37
Frith, W. P.	74
Froude, J. A.	11
Furniture, early Victorian	78, 122
Furniture, Regency	9, 10
Fuseli	73
Gambling	29, 47, 49, 50, 59-69, 89
Gaming House *after* Heath	27
Gaming Room at Crockford's	30
Gaskell, Mrs.	11
Gell, Sir William	76
George III	41
George IV	2, 6, 7, 8
" portrait	17, 26, 40, 41, 42
" at the theatre	49
" his Coronation	61, 62, 89, 103, 104, 114, 115
Gillray	12
Goldsmith, Oliver	79
Gothic Revival, the	16, 17
Gow, Niel	51
Grammont, Duc de	54

125

INDEX

	PAGE
Greenwich Fairs	101
Greville, Charles	47, 48, 90, 104
Grimaldi	85, 94
Gronow, Captain, *quoted*	50, 51, 64, 66, 106, 107
"Guinea-pigs"	32
Gunnersbury House	48
Haberdashers' Almshouses	16
Handicrafts	77
Havell, R., "Sport and Politics"	65
Haydon, R. B.	72, 73
Hayter, Sir George	71
Hazlitt, William	75
Health Resorts	110, 122
Heath, W. Gaming House	27
" Shopping in Bond Street	38
" Tandem-driving and Buying a Horse	40
" Kean as Richard II	49
Hobbyhorse Mania, the	53
Holland, Henry	31, 32
Holland, James	71
Holland, Lady	43, 44
Hook, Theodore	33, 25, 43
Hughes, "Ball"	26
Hunting	119
Illustrators of Books	74*ff*
Ingelow, Jean	11
Islington Spa	94
Jersey, Lady	51
"Jerusalem Chamber," the	60
Jockey of Norfolk, the	30
Jones, Traffic at the Elephant and Castle	68
Kean, Charles	11
Kean, Edmund	11
" as Richard II	49

	PAGE
Kemble, Charles	54
Kemble, John Philip	11
Kenwood	48
Kingsley, Charles	11
Lade, Sir John	6, 29
Lamb, Charles	78, 80
Landor, W. S.	80
Landscape-painting	11, 70*ff*
" examples of	42
Landseer, Sir Edwin	70
Lane, Theodore, Coffee-house	27
" George IV conducted to Royal Box	49
Laurence, S., portrait of Thackeray	43
Lawrence, Sir Thomas	11
" portrait of Queen Caroline	63, 71
Laws, Gaming	59, 63, 67
Lee, Jack	26
Leech, John	12, 74, 101
Leslie, C. R.	42, 70, 74
Lever, Charles	81
Lieven, Princess	51
Lind, Jenny	83
Linnell, James	71
Liszt, F.	46
Literature	11, 78-82
Lock's hat-shop	28
London, Apsley House	105
" Belgravia	18, 20
" Bond Street	27, 28
" Bow Street Runners	61
" Brandenburg House	48
" Bridges	99
" Buckingham Palace	21
" " crowd attending at	29
" " in 1842	34, 40
" Carlton House	6, 14, 15, 22
" " entrance to	31
" " interior	32, 40, 41
" Charing Cross, *after* Moore	4
" *after* Boys	15

INDEX

	PAGE
London, Covent Garden Market	58
,, Covent Garden Theatre, an Entr'acte	47
,, Devonshire House	42
,, Drury Lane Theatre, green room	49
,, Egyptian Hall, the	102
,, Eighteenth Century represented in	23
,, Election Incidents	56
,, Fairs of	100
,, General Post Office	108
,, ,, Mails leaving	80
,, Gore House	32, 34, 39ff, 46, 43
,, Hanover Square Rooms	54
,, Hippodrome	90, 91
,, Last steeplechase at	52
,, Holland House	6, 7, 10, 39ff, 43, 44, 46
,, Houses of Parliament (Old), burnt	15
,, Hungerford Market	58
,, Hyde Park, entrance to	2, 7
,, ,, " Five O'Clock in "	26
,, ,, Society in	37
,, ,, Peace Celebrations	55
,, ,, Troops reviewed (1814)	79
,, Lansdowne House	42
,, Limited development of	18, 19, 20
,, Lonsdale House	48
,, Mansion House, after Boys	14
,, Maps of, early	20, 21
,, Market Gardens in	19
,, Market Scenes	58
,, National Gallery	76
,, Newgate	9
,, Northumberland House	15
,, " No. 1 London "	105
,, Nuisances, after Dighton	6

	PAGE
London, Old Brompton Road, after Scharf	12
,, Paddington Canal opened	79
,, ,, Village of	20
,, Pantheon Bazaar after Richardson	5
,, Pantheon, masquerade at	48
,, Peerless Pool, the	95
,, Piccadilly Gates	1
,, Regency Style in	14, 18
,, Regent Street, from Piccadilly	7
,, ,, towards the Quadrant	14, 14, 22, 15
,, St. Martin's Street	89
,, St. Peter's Church, Eaton Sq., after Waller	12, 15
,, St. James's Park	7
,, ,, Place	42, 43
,, ,, Street	28, 31
,, Shopping in Bond Street	38, 39
,, Social Centres	39-48
,, Society and Writers	79
,, Southwark Bridge, steamers near	60
,, Street Fighting	11
,, Street Scenes: arrival of the Mails	67
,, Election incidents	56
,, Guests to and from Drawing-Room	29
,, Traffic in 1829	28
,, and in 1820	68
,, Tea Gardens	93, 94, 109
,, Tea Merchant's shop	5
,, Town Houses	8
,, Traffic congested	28, 68
,, Wedding, fashionable	16
,, West End, development of	18
,, Western Exchange, the	39
,, White Conduit House	95

INDEX

	PAGE
London, Willis's Rooms	54, 55
Louis Napoleon, Prince	64
"Low Society"	50
Luttrell, Henry	6, 43
" quoted	57
Lytton, Bulwer	33
" portrait *after* Maclise	35, 78
Macall, William	49
Macaulay, Lord	54, 78
Maclise, Daniel, portraits of Lytton and Disraeli	35, 74
Macready, J.	46
Mails arriving in Piccadilly	67
Mails held up	68
Mail Coaches leaving G.P.O.	80
Malibran, Madame	11
Malton, T., St. James's Street	31
Manchester	110
Manners, Lord	26
Margate	119
Martineau, Harriet	54
Masquerade	48
Melton	119
Million Act, the	16
Milnes, Monckton	33, 46
Miniature painting	75
Moberley, Mrs.	57
Money-lenders	60, 67
Moore, Thomas, *quoted*	52
Morgan, Lady	47
Moses, H., "Indoor occupations"	21
Mother of Pearl inlay	120
Müller, W. J.	71
Mulready, William	74
Music	82-84
Nash, Beau	112
Nash, Joseph, Banquet in Brighton Pavilion	1
" Concert	72, 16, 20
Nasmyth	70
Nassuck Diamond, the	55
National Gallery, London	76

	PAGE
Nattes, J. C., Bath	70
" Pump Room	71
Niepce	72
Newmarket	90
Northcote	73
Nixon, John, Worthing Sands	74
Onslow, Tommy	6, 29
O. P. Riots, of 1809	86
Orleans Club, the	56
Osborne, Bernal	33, 46
Paganini	83
Palmerston, Lady	48
Panoramas	102
Pasta, Madame	47
Parrott, W. Chelsea Embankment	13
" Pleasure Steamers S'wark Bridge	60
Patent theatres abolished	88
Peace celebrations	55
Peel, Sir Robert	8
Penny Postage	11
Petersham, Lord	6, 28
Phillip, J., portrait of Turner	44
Photography	72, 75
Pigeon-shooting	98
Pillory, the	9
Pitt, William	113, 31, 32
Place, Francis	37
Poets of the period	80
Police	38
Pollard, James, Settling day at Tattersall's	23
" Betting ring at Epsom	52
" Four-in-Hand Club	66
" Arrival of Country Mails	67
" Louth Mail held up	68
" The G.P.O. in 1830	80, 108

INDEX

	PAGE
Portrait painting	71
Poynter, Ambrose	17
Press-gang	10
Prima Donnas of the '30's	47
Prince's Club	18
Printing	82
Prize-fighting	30, 50, 3, 5, 87, 88, 89
Prout, Samuel	11
Provincial Life	110-122
Provincial Health Resorts	73, 74, 75, 76
Punishments	9, 10
Quadrille	11a
" first introduced	51
Racing	54, 90, 111, 118, 119
Raeburn, Sir Henry	11, 71
Raggett, George	63
Raikes	66, 67
Railways	8, 30, 106, 111
Ranelagh	4, 96
Regatta-time at Cowes	76
" at Dover	75
Regency style, in clothes	3
" furniture	9, 10, 12, 13, 22
Repton, J. S.	16
Reynolds, Sir Joshua, portrait of George IV	17
Richardson, C. J. Pantheon Bazaar	5
Riding, popularity of	33, 34
Rivers, Lord	62
Roberts, David	71
Robinson, W. Crabb	3
Rogers, Samuel	42, 43
Romans à Clef	80
Romney, George	11
Rothwell, R., portrait of Balfe	45
Rosherville Gardens	4, 98
Rouge et Noir introduced	69
Royal Society Meeting, after Walker	46
Rowlandson, Thomas	12
" "low society"	50
" Card Party	27

	PAGE
Rowlandson, T., and Pugin, Preacher at St. Margaret's	16
Performances at Sadler's Wells *and* the Pantheon	48
Rush, Richard, *quoted*	55
Ruskin, John	11, 75
Sadler's Wells	3
" stage spectacle at	48, 85, 94
Sampler, stitched	77
Scharf, George, Tea Merchant's shop	5
" Charity Bazaar	55
" Old Covent Garden Market	58
Scott, General	64
Scott, Sir Walter, portrait *after* Chantrey	44, 11, 23, 78
Seaside Resorts	76, 119
See also Health Resorts.	
Sefton, Lord	6, 14
Shaw, James	17
Shepherd, T. H.,	23
" Gore House	34
" Chiswick House	36
Sheridan, R. B.	11, 66
Siddons, Mrs.	11
Silhouettes, *after* Crowhurst	17, 72
Singers	47, 83
Smirke, Sir Robert	17
Smith, J. T.	23
Smith, Sydney	6, 24, 29, 33, 39, 40
" portrait *after* Briggs	45
Snow Scene	68
Spohr, Louis	83
Sponging Houses	93
Steam-boats, pleasure	60, 99
Steam Yacht, at Spithead	79
Steeplechasing	52
Stephanoff, P., Coronation of George IV, etc.	61, 62
Strawberry Hill Sale	106
Street lighting	94

INDEX

	PAGE
Talbot, Fox	72
Talleyrand, Prince de	33
Tattersall's, Settling day at	23, 29
,, in 1823, by Heath	40
Tax on hair powder	32
Telegraphy	11
Tennyson, Alfred, Lord	11, 78
Thackeray, W. M.	11, 13, 33
,, portrait *after* Laurence	42, 45, 54, 56, 57, 75, 78, 81, 101, 118
Thames, frozen	9
Theatres	3
,, scenes at	47
,, interiors of	48, 49
,, at Cremorne	59, 84-86
,, in Manchester	110, 111
Tickner, George, *quoted*	52, 53
Travelling carriage	64
Trelawney, George	46
Tunbridge Wells	119, 120
Turner, J. M. W.	11
,, portrait *after* Phillip	44, 70
Turnpikes	1
Tussaud, Madame	102
Ude	61, 62
Vauxhall	4, 20, 96, 97
Vestris, Madame	85
Victoria, Queen	7
,, portrait *after* Sully	63
Victoria, Queen, her steam yacht at Spithead	79, 86, 103, 104, 106, 119
Vulliamy, Lewis	17
Wagner, Wilhelm, in London	83
Walker, W., Royal Society Meeting	46
Wallace, Vincent	82
Waltz introduced	51
Ward, E. M.	74
Watts, Joseph	95
Wellington, Duke of	2
,, in Hyde Park	33, 40, 46, 50, 52
,, as High Constable	62, 104, 105
West, Benjamin	73
Wigs	32
Wilkie, David	8, 11, 73
William IV	103, 104
Wilson, Richard	70
Wits, rise of the	28, 29
Women writers	11
Wordsworth, William	11, 78
Worthing	74, 119
Yachting	119
York, Duke of, silhouette portrait	17
York Races	118
Zoological Gardens	102

www.ingramcontent.com/pod-product-compliance
Lightning Source LLC
Chambersburg PA
CBHW080549230426
43663CB00015B/2764